NATIONAL DEFENSE RESEARCH INSTITUTE

T0308507

Drivers of Long-Term Insecurity and Instability in Pakistan

Urbanization

Jonah Blank, Christopher Clary, Brian Nichiporuk

Prepared for the Office of the Secretary of Defense

For more information on this publication, visit www.rand.org/t/rr644

Library of Congress Cataloging-in-Publication Data is available for this publication.
ISBN: 978-0-8330-8750-8

Published by the RAND Corporation, Santa Monica, Calif.

© Copyright 2014 RAND Corporation

RAND® is a registered trademark.

Preface

Pakistan is already one of the most urbanized nations in South Asia, and a majority of its population is projected to be living in cities within three decades. This demographic shift is likely to have a significant impact on Pakistan's politics and stability, but the political and security implications of Pakistan's urbanization remain underanalyzed. This report provides a brief examination of urbanization as a potential driver of long-term insecurity and instability, with particular attention to the cities of Karachi, Lahore, and Quetta.

This report should be of interest to researchers investigating topics including South Asian security, political developments in Pakistan, and the sociopolitical effect of urbanization. The research and analysis contained in this report reflect the political situation through June 2014: As this document was prepared for publication, the late-summer protests led by Pakistan Tehreek-e-Insaf chairman Imran Khan and cleric Muhammad Tahir-ul Qadri held the potential to alter the political balance in Pakistan—but at the time of publication, the outcome of these protests remained in doubt.

The research underlying this report was sponsored by the Office of the Secretary of Defense for Policy and conducted within the International Security and Defense Policy Center of the RAND National Defense Research Institute, a federally funded research and development center sponsored by the Office of the Secretary of Defense, the Joint Staff, the Unified Combatant Commands, the Navy, the Marine Corps, the defense agencies, and the defense Intelligence Community under Contract W91WAW-12-C-0030.

For more information on the International Security and Defense Policy Center, see http://www.rand.org/nsrd/ndri/centers/isdp.html or contact the director (contact information is provided on web page).

Contents

Figures

Tables

Executive Summary

Increasing urbanization is a prominent feature of Pakistani life, with underappreciated implications for the nation's future politics and stability. Already one of the most urbanized countries in South Asia, Pakistan is expected to shift from majority rural to majority urban within the next two to three decades. This phenomenon is highly concentrated. Most of the urban population growth is centered in Pakistan's ten largest cities, and most of that is centered in Punjab. The megacity of Karachi (in Sindh) is in a category of its own: Larger than the next three to four cities combined, with an inflow of Pashtun migrants that challenges the Mohajir-Sindhi balance of the past, it is experiencing greater demographic changes than any other large urban center. The impact of Pakistani urbanization extends far beyond its cities: Thanks to the "floating population" of residents who move to the cities for work but maintain close ties to their ancestral villages, the political and ideological trends of urban Pakistan are spread even to rural areas. As with any social shift, these changes have implications for U.S. security interests. These trends are visible in the three cities examined in this report (Karachi, Lahore and Quetta), and include

- increased demand for (and anger over the lack of) government services (education, clean water, electricity, medical facilities)
- increased exposure to religious ideologies more extreme than the Barelvi and other moderate forms of Islam that most Pakistanis traditionally practice; these include stricter interpretations of Deobandi ideology and Salafi Ahl-e Hadith ideologies imported to Pakistani cities from Saudi Arabia and the Gulf emirates

- increased dissatisfaction with the two major political parties, and perhaps with party politics more broadly.

Even when urban life is superior to rural life, such as in the provision of government services, the availability of information and the ease of organizing collective action (such as protest) means it is easier for urban residents to articulate political demands than it is for their rural counterparts.

Urbanization is already changing Pakistani politics and will continue to do so. The two most important political parties, the Pakistan Muslim League–Nawaz and the Pakistan People's Party, rely on rural vote-banks that are often controlled by feudal interests. These vote-banks will shrink as Pakistan urbanizes, but a potent spoils system and a first-past-the-post electoral structure help entrench the established parties. Despite growing popular disenchantment with both parties, all potential political rivals face serious demographic, ideological, or organizational challenges of their own. The challenge for entrenched parties is to accommodate extant elites while adjusting to new demands. The challenge for new actors is to overcome the tremendous resource advantages the entrenched parties enjoy. Widespread disappointment with political parties and governance will create incentives for change, but incumbent actors have many tools to resist such pressures. Given strong inertial tendencies in Pakistani politics, it seems more likely than not that the current Pakistan Muslim League–Nawaz and Pakistan People's Party structure will survive the pressures of urbanization.[1] The most likely scenarios are that urbanization will change but not transform Pakistani politics.

From a U.S. security perspective, urbanization trends in Pakistan suggest the following conclusions:

---

[1] This analysis is based on developments through June 2014: As this document went to press, the Pakistan Tehreek-e-Insaf was engaged in protests against the government of Prime Minister Nawaz Sharif; the lasting impact of this political conflict, including the potential for Pakistan Tehreek-e-Insaf to replace the Pakistan People's Party as the major long-term threat to Pakistan Muslim League dominance, remained undetermined at time of publication.

- *Increasing urbanization may fuel anti-American sentiment in the near term.* Urbanization is often accompanied by increased access to national and international news. In Pakistan, news about the United States typically focuses on inflammatory topics, such as drones, Guantanamo, and conflict in the Middle East.
- *Increasing urbanization may fuel radical transnational Islamist groups.* Pakistanis working in large cities are exposed to forms of Islam quite different from the Sufi-inflected practice of their ancestral villages. The Ahl-e Hadith ideology that Lashkar-e-Taiba propagates, for example, is considerably more radical than the traditional Deobandi or Barelvi strands of the faith.
- *Increasing urbanization is likely to change the dynamic of counter-terrorism.* In recent years, the locus of U.S. counterterrorism operations has often been lightly settled areas in the Federally Administered Tribal Areas. The type of counterterrorism operations favored in rural areas (particularly drone strikes) is virtually impossible in an urban setting, where the tactics and strategy required are far different.
- *Demographic shifts are likely to make Karachi a potential site for increased terrorism and anti-American extremist operations.* The prevalence of political violence in Karachi is hardly new, and as the megacity continues to expand, it will provide fresh opportunities and sanctuaries for both criminals and terrorists.
- *Demography and urbanization are unlikely to bring Islamist parties to power at the center or in Punjab and Sindh.* To date, urbanization has not resulted in significant electoral success for Islamist parties in the most populous and politically important parts of Pakistan. In terms of security impact, victory by Islamist parties would not necessarily translate to radical shifts in policy: Ideology might be balanced by political expedience.
- *Demography and urbanization are likely to increase demand for political reform.* While rural citizens might have suffered poor governance in silence, their urbanized children are less likely to do so. In the near term, demand for accountability decreases the ability of Pakistani leaders to pursue policies (such as tacit support for U.S. drone strikes) that are highly unpopular. In the long

term, however, the trend may prove beneficial to U.S. security interests: Much of the anti-American sentiment in Pakistan can be seen as a redirection of popular anger flowing from political disenfranchisement and poor governance. The reform movement is a Pakistani response to a Pakistani problem—but one from which the United States may eventually be a collateral beneficiary.

Acknowledgments

The authors are very grateful to the Office of the Secretary of Defense for Policy for sponsoring the research on which this report is based and, most particularly, the officials currently or previously working there who served as project liaisons: Siddharth Iyer, Peter Lavoy, Thomas Greenwood, Kristen Currie, Jessica Cox, David Knoll, Andrew Reeves, and Jennie Guttery. We would also like to thank Daanish Mustafa and Amiera Sawas of King's College, London, whose draft paper presented to the UK Cabinet Office served as a jumping-off point for the work that resulted in this report.

The reviewers of this document, Paul D. Miller and Arif Rafiq, provided invaluable comments, critiques, and guidance, as did our colleagues Eric Peltz and Seth Jones. Their sharp eyes and astute input greatly improved the quality and impact of this report. The authors would also like to express appreciation to our other RAND colleagues who assisted in shaping and preparing this report, including Olga Oliker, Gina Frost, Amanda Hagerman-Thompson, and Joy Merck.

Any errors, of course, are our fault alone—but whatever insights might prove valuable in the pages that follow are the product of a much broader effort.

Abbreviations

ANP	Awami National Party
FATA	Federally Administered Tribal Areas
IRI	International Republican Institute
ISI	Inter-Services Intelligence
JI	Jamaat-i Islami
JUI-F	Jamaat Ulema-e-Islam Fazlur
KPK	Khyber Pakhtunkhwa
MMA	Muttahida Majlis-e Amal
MQM	Muttahida Qaumi Movement
MWM	Majlis Wahdat-e-Muslimeen
PMAP	Pakhtunkhwa Milli Awami Party
PML	Pakistan Muslim League
PML-N	Pakistan Muslim League–Nawaz
PML-Q	Pakistan Muslim League–Quaid-i-Azam
PPP	Pakistan People's Party
PTI	Pakistan Tehreek-e-Insaf
UK	United Kingdom
UN	United Nations
UNHCR	United Nations High Commissioner for Refugees

CHAPTER ONE

Introduction

Origin and Focus of Project

Pakistan is the most urbanized nation in South Asia and has been growing steadily more urbanized for at least the past four decades.[1] The impact of urbanization on Pakistan's politics, stability, and security profile has been underexamined by analysts and policymakers alike. This project attempts to fill a portion of this gap and to focus on how Pakistan's urbanization (and related demographic changes) might shape that nation's political parties, democratic development, and potential security challenges.

This project had its genesis in consultations between the U.S. Office of the Secretary of Defense for Policy and its counterparts in the United Kingdom (UK) Cabinet Office. It was originally envisioned as a collaborative effort between a UK-based research team and a U.S.-based research team, with the two teams working in conjunction and jointly crafting a single document that would be briefed to both the Office of the Secretary of Defense for Policy and the Cabinet Office.

---

[1] The island-nation of Maldives is more urbanized than Pakistan, but the entire population of this state (338,000) is exceeded by at least 15 Pakistani cities. According to United Nations (UN) figures, the percentage of Pakistan's population living in cities exceeded those of all other South Asian nations except Maldives in 2010 and is expected to exceed all except Maldives and the tiny Himalayan kingdom of Bhutan to the end of the projection scale in 2025. (The urban percentages for 2010 were Maldives, 40.0; Pakistan, 35.9; Bhutan, 34.8; India, 30.9; Bangladesh, 27.9; Afghanistan, 24.8; Nepal, 16.7; Sri Lanka, 15.0). (Unless otherwise indicated, all UN Population Division data cited in this volume were gathered from one of three UN databases: "On-Line Data: Urban and Rural Population," "On-Line Data: Urban Agglomerations," and "On-Line Data: Country Profiles" in 2014.)

Subsequent consultations led to a revised approach: The two teams worked sequentially, with each team responsible for its own analysis and conclusions. The UK team, Daanish Mustafa and Amiera Sawas of the Department of Geography at King's College, produced a draft document.[2] While we gained valuable insights from the King's College document, we are solely responsible for this report's content, data, and analysis.

Research Question, Design, and Approach

The basic question this report seeks to explore may be summarized briefly: What are the most salient observations about Pakistan's urbanization, in relation to the nation's electoral politics, likelihood of governmental stability or reform, and security challenges directed at both domestic and global targets?

In designing an approach to examine this question, we sought the most current and reliable data on which to base our analysis. The scarcity of data that are reliable, up to date, and comparable between different population centers presents challenges to any researcher attempting work on the subject. In selecting data on which to base its analysis, we noted that Pakistan's urbanization has been concentrated mostly in about ten cities with populations of more than 1 million; this top-ten concentration is true for both overall population and growth in population. We also noted that the effect of "floating urban populations" and Pakistanis working overseas are understudied aspects of the impact of urbanization on Pakistani politics.

To paint a more-detailed picture of Pakistan's urbanization, we decided to move from nationwide generalities down to a more specific local focus. In choosing which cities to examine, one choice was inevitable (Karachi); one would have been noteworthy if omitted (Lahore); and one was selected to give representation to smaller urban centers

---

[2]   Daanish Mustafa and Amiera Sawas, "Urbanization and Political Change in Pakistan: Exploring the Known Unknowns," draft, London: King's College, 2012.

facing different demographic changes from those the two powerhouses face (Quetta).

The aim of this report is to outline and briefly examine several key trends in Pakistan's urbanization, not to document or demonstrate such trends in authoritative detail. A truly authoritative study of urbanization in Pakistan would require *more* data, more *reliable* data, and more *recent* data than is publicly available. The collection and publication of such data would represent a valuable contribution to scholarship and policy formulation alike.

In security terms, the report concludes that urbanization may fuel anti-American sentiment and help recruitment by transnational Islamist groups (but not necessary Islamist political parties) in the near term, that it is likely to change the tactics and strategy of counterterrorism operations in Pakistan, and that Karachi is likely to become an increasingly significant focus of security threats. It also concludes that urbanization is likely to increase popular demand for political reform, which may temporarily degrade the ability of governments in Islamabad to cooperate with aspects of the U.S. counterterrorism agenda (particularly in such areas as drone strikes) but may well serve to reduce popular anti-American hostility in the long term.

Structure of the Document

Chapter Two discusses the increase in urbanization, the concentration of urbanization in a small number of cities and in the provinces of Punjab and Sindh, the fluid floating population that migrates between urban and rural areas, and the phenomenon of the Pakistani diaspora working in the Middle East (particularly the Gulf States) as a de facto Pakistani "city." The chapter also examines the "draw" factors—including education and medical care—pulling rural Pakistanis into the cities, despite overcrowding, difficult employment prospects, and other challenges.

Chapter Three looks at three case studies as a means of exploring the experience of urbanization in greater detail. Karachi is by far the largest city in Pakistan, one of the largest in the world; Lahore is the nation's cultural and historic capital and, in many ways, its political focal point as well; Quetta is included in the analysis not for its unique stature (as Karachi and Lahore must be) but as a representative of the dozens of second-rank cities and cities away from the large population concentrations in Punjab and Sindh.

Chapters Four and Five, respectively, look at the electoral and security implications of Pakistan's urbanization. In electoral terms, it examines the impact of urbanization on the two major parties (the Pakistan Muslim League–Nawaz [PML-N] and the Pakistan People's Party [PPP]), one new entrant to the top-rung field in 2014 (Pakistan Tehreek-e-Insaf [PTI]), two long-successful regional parties facing challenges from the demography of Pakistan's urbanization trends (the Muttahida Qaumi Movement [MQM] and the Awami League Party), the Islamist parties (particularly the Jamaat-i Islami (JI) and Jamaat Ulema-e-Islam Fazlur (JUI-F), and a cobbled-together party perhaps on its pathway to extinction (the Pakistan Muslim League–Quaid-i-Azam [PML-Q]). Chapter Six summarizes the overall analysis and offers observations about what is likely for the future.

The appendix provides a list of the 50 most populous cities in Pakistan, with current and projected population figures.

CHAPTER TWO

Urbanization Trends in Pakistan

Urbanization Is Increasing

Urbanization is no recent phenomenon for Pakistan: It has been a steady trend since at least 1971 and quite likely since independence in 1947.[1] The UN projects that this trend will continue and even accelerate in the coming years (see Table 2.1). The urbanized percentage of Pakistan's population grew 4.1 percent in the five years between 2005 and 2010 and is expected to grow 4.7 percent between 2010 and 2015. It is expected to grow 10 percent in the decade following 2010, compared with just under 9 percent in between 2005 and 2015.

Whether one looks at the data solely for the period of 1972 to the present or includes both the less-comparable data from 1947 through

Table 2.1
Urban Versus Rural Population

	2005	2010	2015	2020
Rural population (M)	103.9	111.3	118.4	124.1
Urban population (M)	54.7	62.2	71.2	81.2
Percentage urban	34.5	35.9	37.6	39.5

SOURCE: UN Population Division data, accessed November 29, 2013.

[1] Nationwide comparisons stretching further back than 1971 must be taken with extreme caution, since growth in urbanization rates post-1971 must be controlled for the loss from the data set of approximately one-half of the nation's population—a populace in the former East Pakistan that was overwhelmingly rural.

1971 and the projections for trends into the future, the picture remains very similar: A steadily increasing percentage of the population is concentrated in Pakistan's cities, with this percentage likely to become an absolute majority around 2040 (see Figure 2.1).

Urbanization Is Concentrated in a Small Number of Very Large Cities

Most of Pakistan's urban expansion has been concentrated in approximately ten cities with populations above 1 million: Together, these cities constitute more than one-half of the total urban population of the nation.[2] These largest cities are also expanding rapidly. The UN estimates that, by 2015, Pakistan's urban population will have grown by 16.5 million people since 1995; of those, 10.1 million will have migrated to or been born in Pakistan's ten largest cities. This greatly

Figure 2.1
Trends in Urban and Rural Populations

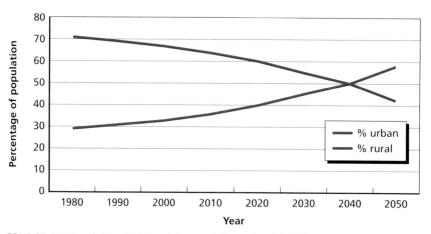

SOURCE: UN Population Division data, as of November 29, 2013.
RAND RR644-2.1

---

[2]   The UN estimates that, in 2015, the ten cities with populations greater than 1 million will have a combined population of 39.6 million, while the total for all populations of cities less than 1 million will be 31.6 million. (UN Population Division data as of April 29, 2014.)

simplifies the analytic task of examining the political impact of Pakistani urbanization: The most important data are not spread out over a range of several dozen small and medium-sized cities, each with its own unique set of variables and local characteristics. Instead, the bulk of the relevant data is concentrated in a limited number of places. The ten largest cities in Pakistan contain most of the country's urban population and urban population growth—and the two megacities (Karachi and Lahore) contain the lion's share of both just between themselves. This trend will continue. Pakistani cities are predicted to expand by 21.1 million people between 2015 and 2025, 15.1 million of which will be in the ten largest cities, and among those will be 7.4 million new residents in Karachi and Lahore. Today and in 2015, one in three urban Pakistanis lives in these two cities (see Figure 2.2).

Figure 2.2
Population Growth in Pakistan's Largest Cities, 1981–2025

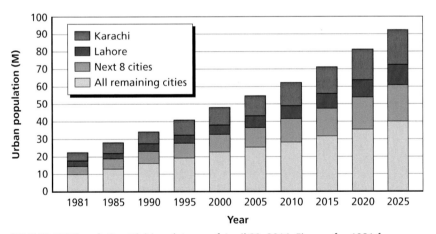

SOURCE: UN Population Division data, as of April 29, 2014. Figures for 1981 from Population Census Organization, Government of Pakistan, "Population Size and Growth of Major Cities," 1998.

Urbanization Is Particularly Concentrated in Punjab, Secondarily in Sindh

Urbanization is more pronounced in Punjab than elsewhere. Of the ten largest cities, six are in Punjab (Lahore, Faisalabad, Rawalpindi, Multan, Gujranwala, and Islamabad[3]). Other than the megacity of Karachi, Sindh has only Hyderabad. In 2008, about one-half of the populations of both provinces were living in cities, while the figures for Balochistan and Khyber Pakhtunkhwa (KPK) were less than 24 percent and less than 17 percent respectively.[4]

Beyond the top ten cities, the Punjabi tilt is even more pronounced: Punjab has 13 of the top 20 cities, 20 of the top 30, 27 of the top 40, and 34 of the top 50 most populous cities in Pakistan. By contrast, Sindh has four of the top 20, six of the top 30, eight of the top 40, and ten of the top 50 cities. For Balochistan, only Quetta sits among the top 50 Pakistani cities, while KPK has five cities among the top 50, with Peshawar being by far the largest.[5]

Urbanization as Fluid Phenomenon: Floating Populations

All urban centers have a floating population of one form or another. In border cities, such as Peshawar and Quetta, many of the residents are migrants (legal or illegal, refugee or longer term) fleeing war or disorder in Afghanistan; 3.3 to 3.6 million Afghans fled into Pakistan prior to 1990. This migration contributed to the near doubling

---

[3] Islamabad is officially a federal district, while Rawalpindi is part of Punjab; in demographic rather than technical terms, the two sites form a relatively seamless urban unit and one that can demographically be described as Punjabi.

[4] Bahrawar Jan, Mohammad Iqbal, and Iftikharuddin, "Urbanization Trends and Urban Population Projection of Pakistan Using Weighted Approach," *Sarhad Journal of Agriculture*, Vol. 24, No. 1, 2008, pp. 173–180.

[5] Rankings from the 1998 census with population totals from Population Census Organization, Government of Pakistan, 1998, and Thomas Brinkhoff, "Pakistan," City Population website, undated.

of the populations of Peshawar and Quetta between 1981 and 1998.[6] Since March 2002, the United Nations High Commissioner for Refugees (UNHCR) has facilitated the voluntary repatriation of millions of Afghan refugees, although the UN still counted 1.6 million registered Afghan refugees in Pakistan as of 2014. Among registered refugees, the UNHCR estimates that 40 percent of Afghan refugees are in refugee camps ("villages" in UNHCR parlance) and 60 percent in Pakistani host communities.[7] These figures likely do not account for a sizable unregistered Afghan population in Pakistan, which a Pakistani cabinet minister assessed might have numbered 1.5 million in February 2014.[8] Many in this pool move back and forth across the Durand Line as opportunities arise. The same is true, to a significant degree, in cities as far away from the border as Karachi.

To what degree does this floating population contribute to politics? If members of this group are refugees, illegal immigrants, or official residents of their ancestral villages rather than of the cities in which they currently live, are they irrelevant to the political power struggles of urban Pakistan? Far from it. There is far more to politics than the casting of ballots—particularly in a country where ballots cast do not necessarily determine political outcomes. Much of the political activity in Pakistan (especially urban Pakistan) occurs completely outside the voting booth. The list of important avenues for effective political participation (generally, but not exclusively, in support of established political parties) includes

- *Street protests.* Mass mobilization was the key mechanism forcing President Pervez Musharraf to yield power in 2008 and has historically been one of the most effective tools for Pakistani citizens

---

[6] Farhat Yusuf, "Size and Sociodemographic Characteristics of the Afghan Refugee Population in Pakistan," *Journal of Biosocial Science*, Vol. 22, No. 3, July 1990, pp. 269–279. The author reports data collected during a January 1989 mission to Pakistan on behalf of UN Population Fund.

[7] UNHCR, "2014 UNHCR Country Operations Profile—Pakistan," 2014.

[8] "Pindi Police Nab 16 Afghan Nationals Under Foreign Act," *Daily Times* (Pakistan), February 24, 2014.

to express their will during periods of de facto or de jure military rule.

- *Fund-raising for political parties.* Lacking any system of public electoral financing, political parties in Pakistan must resort to a variety of fund-raising methods of varying degrees of legality. Traditionally, a relatively small number of patrons have been the primary sources of funding. In recent decades, these cash cows have been supplemented (often, surpassed) by fund-raising from a much wider set of contributors. This has required more supporters—both to provide funds and to solicit them.

- *Land occupation.* Squatting on public or private land can transfer effective control of entire neighborhoods to informal political actors. In Karachi, for example, the establishment of *kachi abadis* [shanty towns] has removed large areas of the city from the de facto jurisdiction of MQM-led municipal authorities and placed these neighborhoods in the hands of Pashtun groups.

- *Crime.* Most political parties (either with or without the approval of their top officials) have at times operated very close to the line separating aggressive financial deal-making and outright criminality. Quite often, they have crossed it. In cities like Karachi, it can be difficult to separate the two: For example, is the MQM a legitimate party that engages in criminal activities to finance its political operation, or is it a mafia that engages in politics to support its criminal enterprises? The same question is all the more salient in the case of parties linked to Taliban factions, both in Karachi and in border cities, such as Quetta and Peshawar.

In all these cases, the participation of the floating population has an enormous bearing on political outcomes. Possession of a valid voter-registration card is hardly a requirement to march in a protest—and many of the illegal or semilegal groups of urban residents are hardly less likely than voting citizens to engage in party-sponsored criminal shakedowns. None of these activities is absent from the countryside, but population density and metropolitan anonymity (among other factors) make them particularly effective in an urban setting.

Pakistanis in Gulf as a Major "City"

An underexamined aspect of Pakistani urbanization is the place of its citizens working abroad. In 2010, 4.7 million Pakistanis were working overseas, 21.5 percent in Saudi Arabia and 20.9 percent in other states of the Persian Gulf according to UN estimates.[9] If the Pakistanis that constitute the diaspora in the Gulf were incorporated as a single metropolis, they would be the sixth largest in Pakistan. The Pakistanis working in the Gulf are living in and absorbing the values of a region steeped in highly conservative Salafi values. How does this experience shape the political leanings of these workers—a population about the size of Rawalpindi or Multan—when they come home? Having provided for their families with remittances and bringing back modest wealth from their time overseas, these individuals likely have more influence than they did prior to their emigration.

Islamist parties, such as the JI and JUI-F, might benefit most from such ideological shifts at the expense of secular ethnic parties, such as the MQM and Awami National Party (ANP), with the center-right PML-N benefiting somewhat more than the center-left PPP. On the other hand, the Salafist version of Islam is less compatible than is generally recognized with the Deobandi and Barelvi schools undergirding JI, JUI-F, and other Islamist parties in Pakistan. The closest ideological match among Pakistani groups might be the Ahl-e Hadith, which has little political party representation but exercises considerable clout outside the electoral framework through the terrorist group Lashkar-e-Taiba and its nominally separate social-service wing Jamaat-ud Dawa. At present, however, little authoritative work has been done in this area. One could make reasonable assumptions about how the experience of residing in a conservative Islamist setting might affect the political choices of nearly 2 million Pakistanis (most of them living

[9] World Bank, "Bilateral Migration and Remittances," *Prospects*, undated. The data record 4,678,730 total Pakistanis overseas, of whom 1,984,647 live in Bahrain, Kuwait, Oman, Qatar, Saudi Arabia, and the United Arab Emirates. In 2010, the UN estimated Rawalpindi as the fifth largest city in Pakistan, with 2.1 million people, and Multan as the sixth largest, with 1.7 million.

in an urban setting while abroad and perhaps when they return), but more work would be needed to form definitive conclusions.

Urbanization, Public Services, and Economic Opportunities

The principal driver of urbanization is unsurprising: No matter how difficult life can be in Pakistan's cities, conditions are even more difficult in rural areas. Three metrics illustrate the point. The first is adult literacy, which serves as a measure of both human capital and access to education. The second is immunization of children between 12 and 23 months for measles, simultaneously a measure of public-service provision and health outcomes. We chose to focus on measles vaccination because it has the lowest reported immunization rate of any major antigen the Pakistan Bureau of Statistics tracks. The third metric is the respondent's perception of the household's economic situation compared to the prior year. Indicators were drawn from the Pakistan Bureau of Statistics' Social and Living Standards Measurement Surveys from 2004–2005, 2008–2009, and 2012–2013.[10]

In adult literacy, Lahore and Karachi are national leaders, while Faisalabad, Peshawar, and Quetta tend to lag (see Figure 2.3). Even so, Faisalabad, Peshawar, and Quetta have adult literacy rates higher than or equal to the provincial averages, with Lahore, Karachi, and Quetta having rates 20 points higher than the provincial totals (see Table 2.2).

The picture is similar for measles vaccination (see Figure 2.4 and Table 2.3). Except for Faisalabad district, the five example cities consistently have higher vaccination rates than the provinces in which they

---

[10] Pakistan Bureau of Statistics, Government of Pakistan, "Pakistan Social and Living Standards Measurement: Brief on Pakistan Social & Living Standard Measurement (PSLM) Survey 2004–15," website, undated. For cities, district-level measurements were taken that include areas classified as urban as well as the rural periphery in the district that contained the urban center. For instance, measurements for Faisalabad contain both Faisalabad city and its adjoining rural areas. This was done both to capture the fluid boundary of South Asian cities and to be conservative in regard to the benefits of city life: If only areas demarcated as urban were measured, the benefits of city life would be even more pronounced than those presented here.

Figure 2.3
Literacy Rates in Key Cities

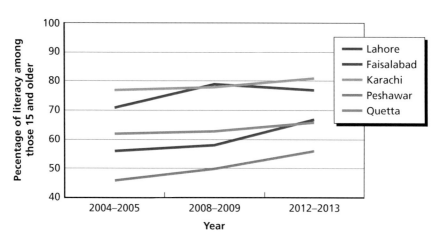

SOURCE: Pakistan Bureau of Statistics, Government of Pakistan, undated.
RAND *RR644-2.3*

Table 2.2
Literacy Rates in Cities Versus Provincial Averages (percent)

	2004–2005		2008–2009		2012–2013	
City (Province)	City	Province	City	Province	City	Province
Lahore (Punjab)	71	51	79	56	77	59
Faisalabad (Punjab)	56	51	58	56	67	59
Karachi (Sindh)	77	54	78	57	81	59
Peshawar (KPK)	46	40	50	45	56	48
Quetta (Balochistan)	62	33	63	39	66	39

SOURCE: Pakistan Bureau of Statistics, Government of Pakistan, undated.

are situated. The differences are most pronounced outside Punjab, due perhaps to Punjab's comparatively high vaccination rates overall.

When looking at literacy and vaccination rates, something else should be apparent: Despite continued urbanization, public services have generally been able to accommodate new migrants. The increases in these indicators since 2004–2005 are modest, and this is more of

Figure 2.4
Measles Vaccination Rates

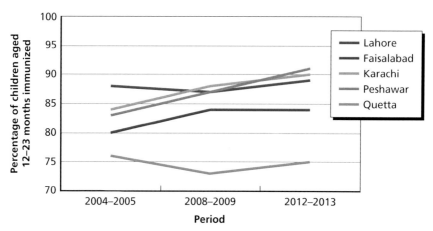

SOURCE: Pakistan Bureau of Statistics, Government of Pakistan, undated.
NOTE: Percentage shown reflects immunization rates according to government
record or caregiver memory. The advantage of living in cities is even stronger if
immunization rates solely based on government records are used as a metric.
RAND RR644-2.4

Table 2.3
Measles Vaccination Rates, Cities Versus Provincial Average (percent)

City (Province)	2004–2005		2008–2009		2012–2013	
	City	Province	City	Province	City	Province
Lahore (Punjab)	88	85	87	86	89	89
Faisalabad (Punjab)	80	85	84	86	84	89
Karachi (Sindh)	84	73	88	70	90	77
Peshawar (KPK)	83	77	87	75	91	77
Quetta (Balochistan)	76	62	73	44	75	55

SOURCE: Pakistan Bureau of Statistics, Government of Pakistan, undated.
NOTE: Data are for vaccinations of children aged 12–23 months.

a case of treading water than rapid improvement. Even so, given the
general negative perception of Pakistani governance, modest improvements are worth emphasizing. Precisely because Pakistan is urbanized,

it has advantages over other South Asian states in providing public services.[11]

When Pakistanis are asked how their households' current economic situations compared to those of one year prior, the same general pattern of urban benefits over provincial averages holds, but the results are far more mixed (see Figure 2.5 and Table 2.4). The difference between the percentage of recipients who reported their situation to be better or much better than the year before and those who said it was worse or much worse is an indicator of whether, on average, individuals perceived improvement in their household's economic well-being. On this indicator, cities experience more variance than their provinces. Smaller units should generally vary more than larger ones, although this might also suggest that a city's residents feel highs and lows more acutely than do rural populations. Even so, the residents of city districts tend to have slightly more optimistic views of their house-

Figure 2.5
Perception of Household Economic Situation

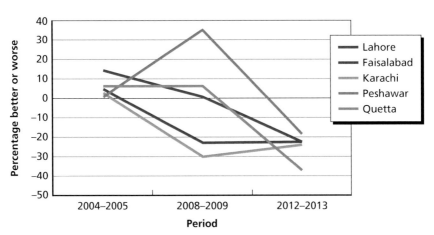

SOURCE: Pakistan Bureau of Statistics, Government of Pakistan, undated.
NOTE: Percentage distribution of households by the perception of the economic situation of the household compared to the year before the survey.
RAND RR644-2.5

[11] Luis Andrés, Dan Biller, and Matías Herrera Dappe, *Reducing Poverty by Closing South Asia's Infrastructure Gap*, Washington, D.C.: The World Bank, December 2013, p. 5.

Table 2.4
Perception of Economic Situation, Cities Versus Provincial Averages
(percent better or worse)

City (Province)	2004–2005		2008–2009		2012–2013	
	City	Province	City	Province	City	Province
Lahore (Punjab)	14	6	1	−8	−23	−18
Faisalabad (Punjab)	5	6	−23	−8	−23	−18
Karachi (Sindh)	3	−8	−30	−25	−24	−16
Peshawar (KPK)	1	1	35	1	−19	−17
Quetta (Balochistan)	6	−5	6	−11	−37	−26

SOURCE: Pakistan Bureau of Statistics, Government of Pakistan, undated.

hold economic situations than do residents of the cities' provinces on average, although this result is largely driven by the relative success of Peshawar and Quetta compared to their provinces in the 2008–2009 data.

Two other results seem evident when scrutinizing household economic perceptions for the past decade. The first is that Karachi residents have been the most pessimistic of the residents of major urban areas. The second is the general negative shift in perceptions over time. The economic growth associated with Musharraf may have been to some extent unsustainable, but it showed up in individuals' economic perceptions in the mid-2000s. The slowing of growth since 2008 is also apparent across the board. While Pakistan's cities continue to beckon millions trapped in a cycle of rural poverty, their promise in recent years has often failed to live up to many residents' expectations.

CHAPTER THREE

Karachi, Lahore, Quetta: A Tale of Three Cities

Karachi: Pakistan's "Maximum City"

Any discussion of urbanization in Pakistan must begin with Karachi—far and away the largest and most economically dominant metropolis in the nation. In 2010, Karachi's population was nearly double that of the next-largest city, Lahore. Apart from Lahore, Karachi is more populous than the rest of the top ten cities combined. Merely the projected growth of Karachi's population from 2010–2020 is greater than the current populations of Multan, Faisalabad, Rawalpindi, and Islamabad put together. (Karachi's 2010 population was 13.5 million, projected to grow 31 percent by 2020 to 17.7 million, an increase of 4.2 million).[1] These estimates may understate Karachi's size, since they all are based on the 1998 census that likely undercounted migrants in the city, such as Afghan refugees. Urban planner Arif Hassan, drawing on the preliminary results of the never-finished 2011 census, concluded that Karachi likely had a population of 21.2 million by 2012, and demographer Mehtab Karim similarly estimated that Karachi's population today might be 22 million, extrapolating from a larger 1998 baseline.[2]

As the nation's financial center, Karachi carries both political and economic weight. Karachi is the country's most important locus of industry and international trade (it is the nation's sole significant port

---

[1] UN Population Division data, November 29, 2013.

[2] Arif Hasan, "The Impending Migration," *Dawn* (Pakistan), December 4, 2012; Mahim Maher, "Demography and Migrations: The Curious Case of Karachi's Ghost Population," *The Express Tribune* (Pakistan), March 29, 2014.

and is likely to remain the trade leader even after the Chinese-built facility in Gwadar becomes fully operational). The status of Karachi's stock exchange, however, puts the city in a category wholly separate from that of other large industrial centers, such as Faisalabad, Multan, and Hyderabad. A 2005 Asian Development Bank report summarized Karachi's unique situation: "The city handles 95 percent of Pakistan's foreign trade, contributes 30 percent to Pakistan's manufacturing sector, and almost 90 percent of the head offices of the banks, financial institutions and multinational companies operate from Karachi."[3] Just as political decisions in Washington are shaped by their expected impact on the New York Stock Exchange, so too are political decisions in Islamabad influenced by whether they are likely to make the Karachi Stock Exchange rise or fall.

Perhaps most important, Karachi has ethnic and sectarian divisions that make its demography a uniquely significant factor in predicting political outcomes. This can be seen in the data of the 1998 census.[4]

Historically, Karachi had been a political arena of contest between Sindhis (the native inhabitants of the state of which Karachi serves as capital) and Mohajirs (descendants of Muslims who migrated from what is now India during the Partition of 1947). Like Mumbai, Chennai, and Kolkata (but not like Lahore and Delhi), Karachi grew from village to city as an entrepôt for colonial trade during British rule in the 19th century. In 1947, its demography radically changed. Almost overnight, such communities as Hindu Sindhis (perhaps two-thirds of

---

[3] Asian Development Bank, *Karachi Mega Cities Preparation Project: Final Report*, Vol. 1, August 2005.

[4] The most recent Pakistani census is now 15 years out of date; the next installment of the census has already been delayed by two years, and there is no firm end date in sight (see Population Census Organization, "Everyone Counts: Census 2011," Islamabad: Government of Pakistan, 2011). The 1998 census data would preferably be supplemented with—or replaced by—more satisfactory information. Unfortunately, no other institution has conducted the sort of comprehensive data gathering about the demographics of Pakistan's key cities that would enable a researcher to forgo the 1998 census. The Pakistani census has historically collected data on "mother tongue," defined as "the language used for communication between parents and the children in the household," but does not collect data on ethnicity. There is often a close correlation between mother tongue and ethnicity (ethnic Punjabis are likely to have Punjabi as their mother tongue), but the two are not coterminous.

the pre-Partition population), Marwaris, Sikhs, and Parsis started to leave, and Muslim Mohajirs from India—primarily from the Urdu-speaking North—arrived *en masse.* The last Pakistani census reported that speakers of Urdu (the lingua franca of Mohajirs) made up 48.5 percent of the population of Karachi (see Figure 3.1).[5] Speakers of Sindhi, by contrast, made up only 7.2 percent—a smaller percentage than those of Punjabi and Saraiki (16.1 percent) and Pashto (11.4 percent).[6] Linguistic preference, however, should not be taken as a perfect proxy for ethnic background: It is likely that some census respondents listing Urdu as their language were of Sindhi ethnicity, regardless of which language they spoke—or which they felt most comfortable telling a census taker they spoke. Perhaps the most noteworthy thing about the language breakdown in the 1998 census is the change it shows since 1981: Urdu speakers declined from an outright majority (54.3 percent)

Figure 3.1
Linguistic Makeup of Karachi, 1998 Census

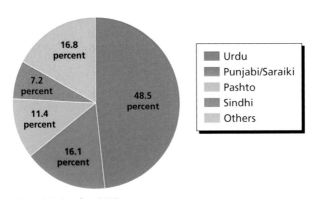

SOURCE: Gazdar, 2013.
RAND RR644-3.1

---

[5] Figures presented are for Karachi division, which encompasses Karachi city and some surrounding areas. Estimates for only what is officially Karachi city fail to capture important areas integral to Karachi politics and economics. The authors are grateful to Haris Gazdar for clarifying this point.

[6] Haris Gazdar, "Karachi Demographic and Politics," presentation of the Urban Resource Center, Karachi, November 6, 2013.

to a mere plurality, while speakers of Pashto and Sindhi increased from 8.7 to 11.4 percent and 6.3 to 7.2 percent, respectively.

Haris Gazdar, assuming differential growth and migration rates among Karachi's linguistic communities, generated estimates for Karachi's demographic landscape in 2011 (see Figure 3.2). His estimates show the continued erosion of the Urdu-speaking demographic position, losing out as Punjabi-, Pashto-, and Sindhi-speaking groups gained population share. As with the 1998 census, Gazdar's estimates are unable to show ethnic changes for individuals that may be ethnically Punjabi or Sindhi but are Urdu-speaking at home.[7]

The Pashtuns represent the fastest-growing segment of Karachi society; they are also a segment of society likely to be underrepresented in government figures. This is due not only to their transience (many Pashtuns working in Karachi maintain ties to their ancestral villages) but also to a political incentive for census workers (often hired by local power brokers) to report an ethnic makeup favorable to the parties in power. The dramatic increase in the number of Pashto speakers tracks closely with the rapid increase in the number of Pashtun residents of Karachi since the start of the anti-Soviet jihad in Afghanistan and continuing during the post-2001 conflicts both inside Afghanistan and in

Figure 3.2
2011 Linguistic Makeup of Karachi, Estimated

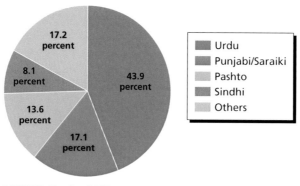

Urdu
Punjabi/Saraiki
Pashto
Sindhi
Others

43.9 percent
17.2 percent
8.1 percent
13.6 percent
17.1 percent

SOURCE: Gazdar, 2013.
RAND RR644-3.2

---

[7] Gazdar, 2013.

the border areas of Pakistan. According to Pakistan government esti-mates, more than 600,000 unregistered Afghans live in Karachi.[8] This number may well undercount the Afghans resident in Karachi and does not include the large number of Pashtun internal migrants driven from Pakistani provinces, such as KPK (until 2008, called the North-west Frontier Province), Balochistan, and the Federally Administered Tribal Areas (FATA). Even taken at face value, the Pakistani govern-ment's reckoning would make Karachi's Afghan population alone one of the 15 largest cities in the nation.

In the 2013 election, MQM took 17 of Karachi's seats in the National Assembly (compared with one each for the PPP, PTI and PML-N). It consistently dominates the city's voting for the provincial assembly, and maintains tight control on municipal power.[9] The 2013 results notwithstanding, the PPP has traditionally been the second-ranking party, due largely to its popularity among Sindhi residents. In 2008, the PPP held three (out of 20) National Assembly seats from Karachi and six (out of 42) provincial assembly seats. The ANP has in recent years been the third most important, with a constituent base almost entirely limited to Pashtun migrants, permitting it to secure two provincial assembly seats in 2008.[10] In 2013, PTI had modest success in Karachi, securing three provincial assembly seats and one National Assembly constituency from Karachi.[11] As demographic currents reach their confluence in Karachi, they have the potential to alter the mix of members of parliament elected from the megacity and its surrounding suburbs. No other area of Pakistan is as electorally meaningful and is simultaneously undergoing such levels of political turmoil.

---

[8]   Khawar Ghumman, "Aliens in Karachi: No Significant Change in Statistics," *Dawn* (Pakistan), February 23, 2014.

[9]   Karachi's municipal structure is constantly changing: Since 1976, it has at various times been a municipal corporation, a collection of zoned municipal committees, five separate municipal corporations, a city district (in 2001), and a single division composed of five dis-tricts (from 2011 to the date of writing). With a few exceptions (such as 2001–2006), the MQM has dominated every configuration.

[10] Azfar-ul Ashfaque, "Impact on Karachi Politics," *Dawn* (Pakistan), December 26, 2011.

[11] Provincial Assembly of Sindh, "Members' List for: Pakistan Tehreek-e-Insaf," 2014; National Assembly of Pakistan, "Pakistan Tehreek-e-Insaf (PTI) Seats Distribution," 2014a.

With ethnic demography playing a greater political role in Karachi than in many other cities (for example, ethnicity is a less salient political factor in more ethnically homogenous cities, such as Multan and Faisalabad), several political conclusions flow naturally from the demographic data:

- MQM, the primary political party representing the Mohajir community of Karachi, is likely to see its dominance of Karachi increasingly challenged. The same trend is likely to affect the MQM's influence in the Sindh provincial power structure and in the national government. The cause for this is simple: MQM (although founded in 1978) arose from a one-time influx of several million Indian Muslims to the state of Pakistan in 1947, and since that single event, the demographic base of the party has expanded only through natural growth of a community with a birthrate slower than those of its neighbors.[12] The only real hope for MQM outreach is to broaden its base in communities underserved by other major political parties, although trendlines appear to be moving in the opposite direction. Karachi's Shi'a population, for example, has been shifting its support *away* from the MQM to the relatively new Shi'a party Majlis Wahdat-e-Muslimeen (MWM). MQM has traditionally competed for the votes of Urdu-speaking middle-class Mohajirs with the Islamist party JI, which had been a dominant force in Karachi politics before the 1980s and won the mayoral elections in 2001 when MQM boycotted the local-body elections.[13] To date, MQM has used its considerable organizational resources to arrest the concomitant decline in political influence that the Mohajir demographic decline portends. Whether the party's resources are sufficient to permit it to transform itself to appeal to new constituencies is an open question. It likely cannot remain influential

---

[12] Anatol Lieven, *Pakistan: A Hard Country*, New York: Public Affairs, 2011, p. 313.

[13] Naimatullah Khan, who served as Karachi's mayor from 2001–2005, was JI's Amir of Karachi from 1990 until his election as mayor; under municipal regulations, he had to resign his party affiliation to serve. In the 2001 elections for the City District Government of Karachi, JI won 12 out of the 20 town *nazim* seats.

in the long term at the national or even provincial level without such an expansion of its base.

While MQM is likely to lose its advantages in Karachi, it is less certain who will be the beneficiary of the party's decline: PPP, PTI, or Pashtun political parties. This uncertainty flows substantially from a lack of recent census data, especially data that distinguish ethnic demographics from linguistic ones. Plausible cases can be made for each of the rival claimants to political power in Karachi.

- Despite its 2013 electoral setback, PPP (as the foremost political vehicle for ethnic Sindhis and a party that has had periodic success in southern Punjab) retains advantages in Karachi. Ever since 1947, a steady influx of Sindhi Muslims has replaced many of the Sindhi Hindus who fled Karachi at Partition, and this rural-to-urban migration is likely to continue in coming years. At a certain point, the trend could be self-reinforcing: As MQM's iron grip on the spoils of power begins to loosen, increasing numbers of Sindhis will enjoy the benefits that come from control of political patronage in Karachi: more no-bid construction contracts, more government jobs, and more opportunities to turn a quick profit. PPP's control of the Sindh provincial assembly will give it resources that other rivals to MQM dominance, such as PTI or ANP, will not have. The more that Sindhis benefit from such perks, the more of them will migrate to the city—and the more that migrate, the greater the power of the PPP will grow vis-à-vis the MQM and other parties.
- Alternatively, the Pashtun population of Karachi has grown even faster than the Sindhi population. Its political power still lags far behind the numbers of its community. Some of this political lag is structural and bound to continue. Many of the Pashtun residents of Karachi are Afghan war refugees, are internal migrants hoping to return to KPK, Balochistan, or FATA if security improves, or are part of the floating population that remains unvested in the political life of the city. Nevertheless, this large and growing Pashtun community is likely to become more politically powerful as its numbers increase. The more secular-minded

of the migrants have bolstered the power of ANP, a Pashtun party with roots stretching back to the pre-Partition Gandhian movement launched by the current ANP president's grandfather, Khan Abdul Ghaffar Khan. Another avenue of political involvement, however, lies in the Pashtun-dominated Islamist party JUI-F, which has traditionally been centered in the border provinces but has seen its influence grow as more Pashtun have moved to Sindh and Punjab. Nominally, JUI-F had 250,000 members in Sindh in 2009–2010, about one-fifth of them living in Karachi; its strongest Sindhi presence is in the Saraiki-speaking districts near the border of Punjab and the Saraiki neighborhoods of Karachi.[14] In practice, JUI-F candidates garnered only 105,799 votes in the 2013 Sindh provincial assembly elections.[15] In addition to competing at the polls, both ANP and JUI-F (as well as a plethora of smaller groups working both sides of the political-criminal dividing line) have engaged in the mercenary aspects of nonelectoral politics so prevalent in contemporary Pakistan.

- PTI achieved moderate success in the 2013 elections in Karachi, winning one national assembly seat and three provincial assembly seats, despite violence that killed one senior PTI party worker in Karachi.[16] Unlike the MQM, PPP, ANP, and JUI-F, PTI is not dependent on any single ethnic constituency and might be able to create a coalition drawing on Karachi's Pashtuns and Punjabis. In the 2013 elections, even though it secured only one national assembly seat, PTI competed well in many constituencies, winning the second largest number of votes behind MQM but ahead of PPP. Even so, unlike MQM, PPP, ANP, and JUI-F, PTI is still a new party that has not shown whether its organization can endure the rigors of Pakistani elections.

---

[14] Joshua T. White, "Conflicted Islamisms: Shariah, Decision-Making, and Anti-State Agitation Among Pakistani Islamist Parties," PhD thesis, Washington, D.C.: Johns Hopkins School of Advanced International Studies, July 2013, p. 332 (for figure of 250,000), p. 339 (Karachi figure, Saraiki districts).

[15] Electoral Commission of Pakistan, "Party Wise Vote Bank," May 27, 2013.

[16] "PTI Senior Leader Killed on Eve of Karachi Polls," *Dawn* (Pakistan), May 19, 2013.

Lahore: Punjab's Heartland

If not for the overshadowing presence of Karachi, Lahore would be the powerhouse of Pakistani cities. With more than double the population of the next most populous city, Lahore has for five centuries been the center of political life in the territory that is now Pakistan. Its population was 7.4 million in 2010 (compared with roughly 3.0 million for Rawalpindi-Islamabad, and 2.9 million for Faisalabad) and is projected to grow 33 percent to 9.8 million by 2020.[17]

Unlike Karachi, Lahore is not an ethnically heterogeneous city. It is a Punjabi city, first and foremost. According to the 1998 census, 85.7 percent of the population is Punjabi, and 11.4 percent speaks Urdu (see Figure 3.3).[18] The ethnic makeup of Lahore has shown considerably less fluctuation over recent decades than have those of Karachi, Quetta, and other more-transient urban areas.

Historically, Lahore has been the bailiwick of the Pakistan Muslim League (PML). During the 1990s, it was the power base of two-time prime minister Nawaz Sharif (who returned for a record third term following the May 2013 elections) and his brother Shahbaz Sharif. During the most recent decade of military rule, between 1999–2008 (first de jure, then de facto), President Pervez Musharraf tried to wrest control of PML from the Sharif brothers by establishing a rival branch, called PML-Q. Taking its name from the honorific title of Pakistan's founding father, Muhammad Ali Jinnah, PML-Q was more often referred to as the "King's Party," with the metaphorical monarch in question being General Musharraf. While in exile in Saudi Arabia after his ouster in 1999, Nawaz reconstituted his base of support as PML-N and seems to have relegated PML-Q to the status of also-ran. (After the 2008 elections, PML-N held 91 seats in the National Assembly, to the PML-Q's 54; following the 2013 polls, PML-N had 129 seats, PML-Q had two.) Absent the support of the military and a few anti-Sharif feudal backers, PML-Q would likely have deteriorated even faster.

---

[17] UN Population Division data, as of April 29, 2014.

[18] Population Census Organization, Statistics Division, Government of Pakistan, *Lahore: Population and Housing Census, 1998*, Islamabad: Government of Pakistan, 2004a, p. 24, Table 2.3.

Figure 3.3
Linguistic Makeup of Lahore, 1998 Census

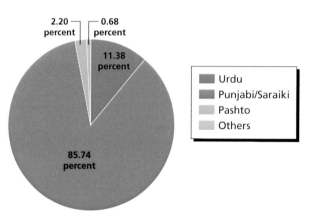

SOURCE: Population Census Organization, Statistics Division,
Government of Pakistan, 2004a, p. 24, Table 2.3.
RAND *RR644-3.3*

PML-N currently holds most municipal, provincial, and national parliamentary seats. PPP's presence in Lahore has never been strong and has deteriorated following a five-year stint of control at the Center, in which the party did little to win the loyalty of new supporters. Parties other than PML-N, such as PPP and the newly invigorated PTI, have little strength in Lahore (or, indeed, in Punjab). As for what the future may hold,

- PML-N is likely to control Lahore and Punjab for the near and medium terms—indeed, until any plausible challenger emerges. Its success is due less to ideology than to a perception (generally well founded) that the party does a reasonably good job of delivering patronage to its core constituents. Since Lahore has always been an overwhelmingly Punjabi city, ethnic demographic patterns will not determine political outcomes. PML-N's case will stand or fall on the basis of results rather than ideology. During his tenure as Punjab's Chief Minister, Shahbaz Sharif has won generally high marks for improvements in the province's educational system. Voters will look to PML-N to demonstrate competence in building and maintaining local infrastructure, along with providing other goods and government services. If it can do so, it will remain the presumptively dominant party for the foreseeable future.

- The elections of 2008 may represent the PPP high-water mark in Lahore, at least in the near future. They were held less than two months after the assassination of PPP leader and two-time prime minister Benazir Bhutto, and her widower Asif Ali Zardari (who soon assumed the mantle of president and controls PPP with a firm hand) received a considerable sympathy vote even from citizens not normally inclined to support his party.

- Neither PML-Q nor PTI, a party led by former cricket star Imran Khan, seems likely to challenge PML-N in Lahore. PTI has a substantial Lahore presence—it was founded in Lahore in 1996 and staged its most noteworthy street protest in Lahore on October 20, 2011 (a rally that reportedly drew 100,000 participants). However, even Imran Khan himself—a longtime resident of Lahore and a hero to the cricket-mad city—has been unable to win a seat from his adopted hometown (in 2013, he won a seat from Rawalpindi; in 2002, he won from Mianwali). Pakistani observers in 2012 noted that, while the PTI generally lacked organization throughout Punjab, it did have some party organization in KPK, putting them on a path to compete with JUI-F for seats.[19] This prediction was borne out in the 2013 polls. The first-past-the-post electoral system (the parliamentary structure whereby seats are won by simple majority or plurality, rather than allotted on a proportional basis) can be cruel for new parties. PTI won nearly 18 percent of the vote for the Punjab Provincial Assembly, but that translated into fewer than 8 percent of the seats. (PML-N won just over 40 percent of the vote, earning it nearly 83 percent of the provincial assembly seats.)[20]

- Islamist parties have had little electoral success in Lahore. Lahore is the only major city in which the country's largest Islamist party,

---

[19] Discussion with Pakistani political analyst and Pakistani journalist, Dubai, April 2012.

[20] Provincial Assembly of Punjab, "Member's Directory: By Party Affiliation," 2014; Electoral Commission of Pakistan, 2013.

JI, has seen even modest electoral success. In the 2002 election (in which the military-backed regime tilted the playing field in favor of the Islamist parties against the secular PPP and PML-N), JI won only two seats in parliament—both from Lahore. The party boycotted the 2008 elections, perhaps fearing a similar showing. In 2013, it did not win any seat from Lahore. Despite the fact that JI has roughly 2.6 million members in Punjab (60 percent of its nationwide membership) and despite the fact that it is headquartered in Lahore, the party has played a much larger roll in the street than in the voting booth. Its nearest Islamist rival, JUI-F, has even less of a presence in Lahore: 150,000 members in Punjab (less than 10 percent of its nationwide total) and no real impact on Lahore's politics.[21] JI and JUI-F candidates garnered 489,772 and 153,398 votes, respectively, out of the 27,875,857 cast in the 2013 Punjab provincial assembly elections.[22] Outside the realm of elections, however, Islamist groups have had considerably more influence. The annual conference of Lashkar-e-Taiba/Jamaat-ud Dawa, held less than 20 miles from Lahore in the town of Muridke, has regularly drawn tens of thousands of participants most years in which it has been permitted to be held. These theoretically banned extremist groups regularly support street protests and other forms of political participation even if they are not directly represented in the polls.

Quetta: View from the Periphery

Quetta just barely makes the list of Pakistan's top ten cities but is indicative of trends in smaller and medium-sized population centers throughout the parts of the country that border Afghanistan. The demography of Punjabi cities, such as Multan, Faisalabad, and Rawalpindi, may mirror those of Lahore to some degree, and Sindhi cities, such as Hyderabad, may follow either Karachi or similar-sized Punjabi

---

[21] Figures from White, 2013, pp. 323, 332.

[22] Electoral Commission of Pakistan, 2013.

cities, such as Gujranwala, but large stretches of urban Pakistan more closely resemble Quetta's demographic picture.

Because of its transient population of refugees from Afghanistan and its floating population drawn both from Balochistan and from FATA, it is difficult to acquire reliable demographic data in Quetta. Its population is probably about at the 1 million mark: It was estimated at 874,000 in 2010, with projected growth of 38 percent to 1.2 million by 2020. That would place it roughly on par with Islamabad (excluding the far larger metropolis of Rawalpindi) and somewhat smaller than the other top-ten border city of Peshawar (1.5 million in 2010, projected growth to 2.0 million by 2020).[23]

The ethnic composition of Quetta's population is rather more difficult to ascertain than those of other large Pakistani cities. Census data are less reliable here than those for Lahore or even Karachi: The ethnic balance has likely changed significantly since 1998 because of the post-2001 developments in Afghanistan, Pashtun insurgencies in FATA and KPK, and a low-intensity Baloch insurgency in Balochistan. The capital of Balochistan does not have a majority of ethnic Baloch, or any linguistic group. According to the 1998 census, Baloch speakers made up a slight plurality of Quetta residents, at nearly 25 percent (see Figure 3.4), followed by Pashto speakers (23.7 percent), and Punjabi/Saraiki speakers (21.7 percent).[24] Other credible sources assessed a modest Pashtun plurality even in 1998.[25]

---

[23] UN Population Division data, as of April 29, 2014.

[24] Population Census Organization, Statistics Division, Government of Pakistan, *Quetta: Population and Housing Census, 1998*, Islamabad: Government of Pakistan, 2003, p. 25, Table 2.3. Even this may overstate the Baloch presence, since "the census does not distinguish Brahui speakers from Baloch speakers, even though the two languages are linguistically distinct and completely unrelated." C. Christine Fair, testimony before the U.S. House of Representatives Committee on Foreign Affairs, Subcommittee on Oversight and Investigations, February 8, 2012.

[25] Citing "Population census reports," Gazdar and colleagues give a different breakdown with a Pashtun plurality: 30.0 percent Pashtun, 27.6 percent Baloch and Brahui, 17.5 percent "Other indigenous to Balochistan," and 25.0 percent "Settler" (mostly Urdu, Punjabi, or Saraiki speakers). Haris Gazdar, Sobia Ahmad Kaker, and Irfan Khan, "Buffer Zone or Urban Hub? Quetta: Between Four Regions and Two Wars," working paper, London: Crisis States Research Centre, London School of Economics, 2010, p. 12.

Figure 3.4
Linguistic Makeup of Quetta, 1998 Census

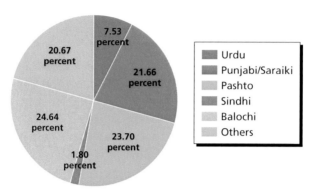

SOURCE: Population Census Organization, Statistics Division,
Government of Pakistan, 2003, p. 25, table 2.3.
RAND RR644-3.4

Whatever the ranking of ethnicities in 1998, a Pashtun plurality—perhaps a sizable one—seems evident today. One telling indicator is that representatives of the Pakhtunkhwa Milli Awami Party
(PMAP), a Pashtun nationalist party strongest in Balochistan, hold
both National Assembly constituencies for Quetta and four of the six
provincial assembly constituencies.[26]

Quetta politics today are an extension of the complicated coalition politics in Balochistan, where PML-N supported PMAP during
the 2013 election. At the provincial level, PMAP is in coalition with
the National Party, a Baloch political party. PMAP holds the governor-
ship, while the National Party holds the chief ministership, a division
of offices that left PML-N demanding the Quetta mayorship for its
role in the coalition. That intracoalition fight between a Pashtun party,
a Baloch party, and a "Punjabi settler" party is indicative of politics in
Quetta, which lacks a majority ethnic group.[27]

---

[26] National Assembly of Pakistan, "Pukhtoonkhwa Milli Awami Party (PMAP) Seats Distribution," 2014b; Provincial Assembly of Balochistan, "By District: Quetta," 2014.

[27] Zia-ur Rehman, "Swing Seats," *The Friday Times* (Pakistan), April 26, 2013; Saleem
Shahid, "PkMAP, PML-N Eye Quetta Mayor's Post," *Dawn* (Pakistan), December 18, 2013;
Saleem Shahid, "Cracks but No Sign of Break-Up," *Dawn* (Pakistan), February 15, 2014.

Also in 2013, Quetta's Hazara population moved away from the secular Hazara Democratic Party to the harder-edged MWM, which may suggest a further polarization of the political space along sectarian lines. It is unclear whether this represents a more-permanent shift for other Shi'a groups, which have lent support to PPP in the past but might cast their lot with MWM in the future if they feel increasingly embattled.

A final factor to bear in mind for any political analysis of Quetta is the role the Pakistani military plays, especially through Inter-Services Intelligence (ISI). Pakistan's spy service is widely believed to have involved itself in the electoral process on many occasions and in many locations throughout the country's history, supporting candidates and parties the military favored and intimidating those the military considered to be dangerous to its institutional interests. This has been a factor in many urban settings but seldom to the degree seen in Quetta. The capital of Balochistan is a garrison city, and the military presence there is both visible and dominant. ISI is believed to have put its finger on the electoral scale in larger urban areas, but it is not seen as having outright dictated the outcome of polling in such megacities as Karachi and Lahore in recent elections. In Quetta (and, to some degree, Peshawar), however, the military has a considerably freer hand. While ISI may or may not choose to intervene in a particular election, it is reasonable to conclude that there will not soon be a political outcome in Quetta to which the Pakistani military strongly objects.

CHAPTER FOUR

The Political Environment

Pakistan Muslim League–Nawaz

At a national level, Pakistan's governing party garnered only 33.3 percent of the votes in the 2013 election,[1] but due to the first-past-the-post electoral structure, this translated to 129 of the 272 directly elected seats in the National Assembly (compared with 34 for PPP and 25 for PTI)[2] and made Nawaz Sharif the prime minister. PML-N's dominance of Punjab has never seriously been challenged, and the party looks set to control Pakistan's most populous province for the foreseeable future: In the 2013 election, it won 214 of 297 seats in the provincial assembly, by far its strongest showing anywhere in the country (by contrast, it won only four of 130 seats in the Sindh provincial assembly, 12 of 99 in KPK, and nine of 51 in Balochistan). In demographic terms, it has not expanded significantly beyond its core constituency of ethnic Punjabis, but this slice of the population is sufficiently large and engaged to ensure that whoever controls it will be at the center

---

[1] Seat counts in Pakistan's national and provincial assemblies are constantly changing: In the May 2013 elections, many candidates ran in multiple constituencies, so by-elections were held to fill vacancies due to cases of multiple wins; in the frantic government-shaping that followed the polls, the PML-N seat count rose as more legislators scrambled to get on board with the new regime. To maintain comparability, the results cited in this section (and throughout the report, except where explicitly noted) refer to seats won by direct election (that is, excluding seats reserved for specific communities, often conferred on a proportional basis), as of the conclusion of vote counting in May 2013.

[2] Figures for 2013 election results cited in this section are taken from the compilation at HamariWeb.com, 2013.

of national power. PML-N retains a firm hand over municipal and parliamentary seats in Lahore and is an equal player in the contest for Quetta, but has no significant power in the megacity of Karachi.

Pakistan People's Party

PPP continues to have the broadest geographic base of any party in Pakistan and is likely to retain this shallow-but-wide level of support despite its current unpopularity and internal leadership transition. It won the second highest number of directly elected seats in the National Assembly (34), but this represents a very serious fall from its 2008 standing. According to the 2013 election results, PPP drew only 15.2 percent support at the national level, lagging behind both its traditional rival (PML-N, which polled over twice as well) and the newly competitive PTI (at 16.7 percent). By way of comparison, in the International Republican Institute's (IRI's) last poll before the February 2008 elections (but conducted before the assassination of Benazir Bhutto, thereby reflecting support for PPP rather than a sympathy vote), PPP outpolled all other parties but still drew support of less than one-third (30 percent) of those surveyed. By this metric, PPP lost one-half of its support during the term of office it completed in 2013 but entered that tenure (as PML-N entered its 2013 term of governance) only as a plurality party at the outset.[3] Sindh continues to be the PPP base: Despite national unpopularity, the party won one-half the provincial assembly seats (65 of 130) and, despite a poor showing in 2013 provincial elections outside of Sindh (six seats in Punjab, two in KPK and none in Balochistan), retains significant pockets of loyal constituents throughout the country. In the three cities examined, PPP's position is soft: It holds one seat in Karachi and none in Quetta and Lahore. Rural Sindh is PPP's firewall, with portions of rural Punjab as a secondary base. Sindhi urban sites other than Karachi (which is MQM's sole seat of dominance) are also PPP territory and likely to remain so.

---

[3]   IRI, "IRI Index: Pakistan Public Opinion Survey," November 19–28, 2007.

Pakistan Tehreek-e-Insaf

In 2011–2013, PTI, a party led by former cricket star Imran Khan, emerged as a vehicle for disaffected citizens to vent their frustrations on both established political parties and on the entire political establishment. According to a 2012 IRI poll, PTI was more popular at a national level than any other party (31 percent support, versus 27 percent for PML-N and 16 percent for PPP) and garnered the support of one-third of those polled in Punjab, 15 percent of those in Sindh (more than MQM or PML-N), and 35 percent of those in Balochistan (more than PML-N or PPP).[4] These results were not borne out in the 2013 elections: PTI won only 16.7 percent of the national votes—a figure second only to that of the PML-N but barely one-half the party's preelection poll numbers and only enough to earn a mere 25 seats in the National Assembly. In the provincial assemblies, PTI won only in KPK, where its 35 seats enabled it to lead a coalition government; it won only three seats in Sindh, 19 in Punjab (its demographic base), and none in Balochistan.

While preelection predictions of a PTI national victory were always implausible, the results represented a genuine shake-up of the established political order in Pakistan. Between its founding in 1996 and the election of 2013, PTI had been a one-man show: The sole National Assembly seat it had ever won had been that of Imran Khan himself—in 2002, from Mianwali. (It is noteworthy that this Lahore-based party had been unable to win a seat in Lahore in for its leader, who contested for seven seats in 2002 and won only in a city of 85,000 in the northwest of Punjab. In that election, PTI won only 0.8 percent of the popular vote).[5] The shift of fortunes in 2013 was partly attributable to a popular distaste for both major parties—but PTI owed a

---

[4] Anwar Iqbal, "PTI Losing Ground Amid PML-N Surge: IRI survey," *Dawn* (Pakistan), September 30, 2012. IRI described its methodology, but refrained from publishing its results: IRI, "Detailed Methodology: Survey of Pakistan Public Opinion, February 9–March 3, 2012," April 23, 2012.

[5] Electoral Commission of Pakistan, "Detailed Position of Political Parties/Alliances in National Assembly General Elections," 2002.

number of its seats to opportunistic defections from PML-N and PPP (including former PPP Foreign Minister Shah Mehmood Qureshi).

Muttahida Qaumi Movement

MQM appears fairly secure in Karachi for the near term, but demographics are working against the party representing Mohajirs. The base of the party is static: It migrated to Karachi (and other cities) in 1947 and 1948 and has since expanded largely through reproduction. After a relatively modest jump following the independence of Bangladesh in 1971, the party's middle-class base of support may well have seen more emigration (to Britain, the United States, Canada, and other foreign countries) than immigration. In Karachi, MQM will continue to serve as a bulwark against the demographic tide of immigration by ethnic Sindhis, Pashtuns, and other groups—but, sooner or later, the tide always comes in. MQM has proven itself to be very effective in the more brutal aspects of street politics (extortion and intimidation, for votes and profit), but with the influx of both hard-bitten Pashtun residents and hard-charging Taliban-linked criminal groups, the Mohajir party may have met its match. It brought in 5.7 percent of the vote in the 2013 election, earning 19 seats in the National Assembly (only eight fewer than PTI). In the provincial assembly of Sindh, it won 37 seats: barely half that of the PPP, but more than five times the seats won by PML-N and PTI combined. MQM won no seats in any other provincial assembly.

Islamist Parties

The two main Islamist parties (JUI-F and JI) together won just under 5 percent of the vote in 2013, which brought them 11 seats in the National Assembly and 20 seats in the provincial assembly of KPK; they won an additional six seats in the Balochistan assembly and one in the Punjab assembly. Near-term demographic trends are unlikely to empower the Islamist parties enough to bring them to power in major urban centers, let alone at the national level. Every attempt to pull the various Islamist parties together into a lasting alliance has thus far proven futile. The Muttahida Majlis-e Amal (MMA) was formed in the run-up to the 2002 national elections; the party received considerable support from the military in this largely stage-managed polling yet managed to garner only 11 percent of the vote and 58 parliamentary seats. That year, they were also bolstered by the anti-Americanism that accompanied the Afghanistan war, a sentiment that increased in 2003 with the Iraq war. Even so, since 2002, the "United Council of Action" has shown itself to be neither united nor a council nor an instrument of action. In the 2008 elections, the MMA failed even to forge agreement between JI and JUI-F, the two most politically potent Islamist movements in the country; due to boycotts by JI and other constituent elements, the MMA has been reduced largely to a shell for the JUI-F. In the three cities examined,

- JUI-F is the politically stronger of the two main Islamist parties: It won 2.8 percent of the national votes and eight National Assembly seats in the 2013 election. But JUI-F remains Pashtun focused, with its center of gravity on the frontier; it won 13 seats in the provincial assembly of KPK and six in Balochistan. It is weak in Lahore and Karachi, although its influence in the latter (as well as in Quetta, where it has greater strength) is likely to grow with increased inmigration from FATA.
- JI is not a significant electoral factor in Karachi, Lahore, or Quetta. Did JI boycott the 2008 elections because it knew the polls would demonstrate its inability to win seats? Or has JI's relatively poor showing in elections when it has participated (2002, for example) been the result of its refusal to engage in patient construction of an effective electoral base? The answer is possibly both. The group has its headquarters and its strongest political influence in Lahore, through street demonstrations and other nonelectoral forms of political action. It brought in only 2.1 percent in the national elections, following closely behind JUI-F, but netted only three National Assembly seats to JUI-F's eight. It also

won seven seats in the provincial assembly of KPK and one in its power center of Punjab.

Awami National Party

The ANP continues to be the primary vehicle of political expression for Pashtuns from tribes and clans resident in KPK and northern Balochistan, but the group's moderate ideology seems increasingly outdated: In the 2013 election, it won only 1.0 percent of the votes, yielding two seats in the National Assembly. It fared poorly even in Pashtun-dominated provinces: four seats in KPK (compared with Punjab-centered PML-N and PTI, which won 12 and 35 seats, respectively) and only a single seat in Balochistan (compared with nine seats for PML-N). ANP's poor showing in 2013 largely involved anti-incumbency sentiment combined with ruthless violence by the Tehrik-e Taliban Pakistan, which killed ANP candidates and impaired the party's ability to campaign widely. It is also possible the ANP is suffering from an ideological shift in which the party's more-secular perspective is no longer congruent with its potential constituents. As more Pashtun youth work in the Gulf or fight in Afghanistan (and as those who do not take these paths increasingly have their views shaped by relatives or friends who do), the attraction of a secularist Pashtun party may well shrink further. In the three cities studied in this report, ANP has a negligible presence in Lahore but more influence in Karachi and Quetta. In Karachi, it has not translated its presence to electoral success, but it has been the dominant voice of a large and growing Pashtun population with roots in KPK. Demographics have historically favored ANP in Karachi: The success of ANP (as opposed, for example, to JUI-F) would seem to owe more to the home province of most Karachi Pashtun (KPK rather than FATA) than to ideology. Whether the ANP can maintain its role as representative of the Karachi Pashtun in the face of TTP violence in Karachi is in doubt.

Pakistan Muslim League–Quaid-i-Azam

In the absence of a military coup (and perhaps even with one), PML-Q appears to be dying: A 0.4 percent showing in the 2013 elections led to two seats in the National Assembly, along with seven seats in the Punjab provincial assembly, one in Sindh, and five in Balochistan. PML-Q remains a party without a clear constituency, leader, or *raison d'etre*—hence, a party unlikely to be helped or harmed by demographic trends, urban or rural. It was unable to displace the Sharif brothers when Nawaz was in exile in Saudi Arabia, even as the party General (and subsequently President) Pervez Musharraf favored. With Nawaz firmly back in his Lahore bailiwick and with Musharraf battling merely to stay out of prison, PML-Q seems to be as much of a spent force as its creator. In Punjab and KPK, the party has been eclipsed by Imran Khan's PTI. The former "King's Party" remains a potential site for the disaffected should PTI fade, as well as a potential vehicle the Pakistani military could use to put a plausibly legitimate civilian face on a de facto military-led regime, if it chose to do so in the future. Absent such backing, it is difficult to see how PML-Q finds a role as anything other than a repository for elite power brokers (especially those in Punjab) opting for "none of the above." These elites have captive voters who will travel with them when another party offers them a better deal than they believe they can receive under the PML-Q umbrella. Some future military strongmen may resurrect the party or something like it, but in the meantime, politicians with real influence who once were members of PML-Q have returned to the open arms of other parties.

CHAPTER FIVE

Security Considerations

From the standpoint of American national security policymakers, the most pressing question about Pakistan's urbanization is what impact (if any) it is likely to have on U.S. security interests. While the impact of urbanization on security is likely to be indirect and while predictions are of necessity speculative, it is possible to draw several observations from the data described in this report.

Increasing Urbanization May Fuel Anti-American Sentiment

As noted above, urbanization in Pakistan corresponds closely with increases in literacy—but not necessarily with perceptions of household economic well-being. This is a potentially volatile combination: greater access to global news and (often) a greater sense of personal hardship. As Pakistan has urbanized over the past decade, perceptions of the United States have gotten increasingly negative (see Figure 5.1). Literate urbanites are more likely than their rural counterparts to have daily access to information about distant events, such as the war in Iraq, prisoner abuse at Abu Ghraib, or detainees in Guantanamo. Even events closer to home, such as U.S. drone attacks inside Pakistan or military action in Afghanistan, reach an urban population more regularly than they reach remote rural villages. The range of global issues that might spur a reaction is virtually limitless: A YouTube video defaming the Prophet, a self-ordained Florida pastor burning a Qur'an, an inflammatory cartoon published in Denmark—all these might have

Figure 5.1
Pakistani Views of the United States

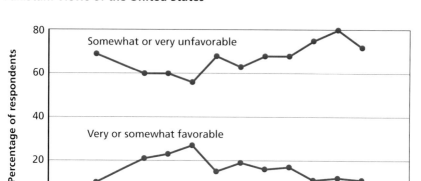

SOURCE: Pew Research Center, Global Attitudes Project, "2013 Spring Survey Topline
Results," May 7, 2013.
NOTE: Question was phrased: "Please tell me if you have a very favorable,
somewhat favorable, somewhat unfavorable or very unfavorable opinion of:
a. The United States."

passed unnoticed in the rural Pakistan of the past. In the near future,
more than one-half of Pakistan's population will be living in cities,
where such provocations dominate news and local conversations. Anti-
American sentiment in Pakistan soared in 2002–2003 as a result of the
Afghanistan and Iraq wars but is likely the same or even higher today.[1]

---

[1]   Pew Research Center, Global Attitudes Project, "Pakistani Public Opinion Ever More
Critical of U.S.: 74% Call America an Enemy," June 27, 2012. In previous decades, the news
reports reaching a predominantly rural population typically came by radio, a medium lacking the immediacy of television or Internet visual imagery and, in Pakistan, generally avoid-
ing controversial topics.

Increasing Urbanization May Fuel Radical Transnational Islamist Groups

The forms of Islam traditionally practiced in most of Pakistan have been politically moderate.[2] Most Pakistanis have followed the Barelvi path, and the form of Deobandi practice has generally been less extreme than that found among many practitioners of today. A solid majority of Pakistanis have sometimes or regularly followed Sufi practices, and *tariqas*, such as the Naqshbandiya, Chishtiya, and Qadiriya, have deep histories. Urbanization and the phenomenon of Pakistan men working in the diaspora "city" of the Gulf have greatly increased Middle Eastern (as opposed to South Asian) forms of Islam, such as the Salafi school. The Ahl-e Hadith school was virtually unknown in Pakistan a few decades ago but has made inroads through Lahore and other cities; it remains largely unknown in most rural areas. These ideologies are often linked to radical movements: The terrorist group Lashkar-e-Taiba, for example, follows the Ahl-e Hadith ideology.

Sunni-Shi'a conflict, while hardly unknown in rural areas, has increased in urban settings. This is in line with social science research about the impact of urbanization on religious and ethnic conflict, both in South Asia and more broadly.[3] Violent sectarian conflict has an outsized importance in Quetta, due both to the significant Shi'a population and to the strength of radical Sunni groups for whom anti-Shi'a ideology is a motivating concern. Terrorist groups, such as Lashkar-e-Jhangvi and Sipah-e Sahaba, are largely Punjab-based but have close ties to the Quetta Shura Taliban and a wide range of other violent extremist groups (such as the Haqqani Network) active in the border areas. Increased Sunni-Shi'a conflict has led to out-migration of Shi'a from Quetta to such cities as Karachi, potentially taking the battles further afield. From a U.S. security perspective, anything that increases

---

[2]   For a discussion of the interplay of traditional Islamic practices and modernist reinterpretations, see Jonah Blank, *Mullahs on the Mainframe: Islam and Modernity Among the Daudi Bohras*, Chicago: University of Chicago Press, 2001. Much of the fieldwork for this study was conducted in Karachi and Lahore.

[3]   For a discussion of this phenomenon in a South Asian context, see Ashutosh Varshney, *Ethnic Conflict and Civic Life*, New Haven: Yale University Press, 2002, pp. 281–300.

the influence of radical Sunni groups (many, like Lashkar-e-Jhangvi, with ties to Gulf-based sponsors of extremism) or radical Shi'a groups (some, like Sipah-e Muhammad, with ties to Iran) must be considered a cause for concern. While sectarian groups may direct their violence toward local doctrinal foes at present, such battles (as the examples of rival Sunni and Shi'a radical groups in Iran and Syria demonstrate) can seldom be neatly segregated from much broader geopolitical conflicts. More concretely, Sunni sectarian groups, such as Lashkar-e-Jhangvi, are believed to have relationships for training, sanctuary, and fundraising with transnational terrorist groups of deep concern to the United States, including Lashkar-e-Taiba, Jaish-e Muhammad, and possibly Al Qaeda. Shi'a counterparts are of less immediate concern to the United States, but the flow of expertise, personnel, and weapons among Shi'a militias in Afghanistan, Pakistan, and the Middle East is often coordinated by Iran's security services.[4]

Increasing Urbanization Is Likely to Change the Dynamic of Counterterrorism

As a simple matter of operational logistics, U.S. counterterrorism efforts in Pakistan will necessarily be affected by urbanization. In recent years, the locus of U.S. counterterrorism operations has often been lightly settled areas in FATA and other border regions. These sites have presented challenges of their own, but when a target has been identified, U.S. drones have been able to launch targeted attacks with considerable accuracy and limited civilian casualties. This mode of operation is virtually impossible in an urban setting: To date, there has been no

---

[4]   For discussion of the threat Lashkar-e-Taiba poses to the United States, see Jonah Blank, "Lashkar-e-Taiba and the Threat to the United States of a Mumbai-Style Attack," testimony delivered to the House of Representatives Committee on Homeland Security, Subcommittee on Counterterrorism and Intelligence, Santa Monica, Calif.: RAND Corporation, CT-390, June 12, 2013. For discussion of linkages between Lashkar-e-Taiba and other militant or terrorist groups in South Asia, see Jonah Blank, "Kashmir: All Tactics, No Strategy," in Sumit Ganguly, ed., *The Kashmir Question: Retrospect and Prospect*, London: Frank Cass, 2003, pp. 181–202; and Jonah Blank, "Kashmir: Fundamentalism Takes Root," *Foreign Affairs*, Vol. 78, No. 6, November/December 1999, pp. 36–53.

publicly documented drone attack on an urban site in Pakistan. All publicly documented counterterrorism operations in Pakistani cities have been conducted by security forces, usually with U.S. and Pakistani teams working together (as was the case in the 2003 capture of Khalid Sheikh Muhammad in Rawalpindi and the 2002 capture of Ramzi bin al-Shibh in Karachi) and very occasionally by U.S. personnel acting without Pakistani knowledge (as was the case in the 2011 raid on Osama bin Laden's hideout in Abbottabad). As more of the Pakistani population moves to cities—and as Pakistani cities become increasingly attractive sites for terrorists to take refuge—U.S. counterterrorist operations will accordingly shift to urban settings.

Pakistan's own counterterrorism resources will be further strained by increased urbanization. The resources necessary for urban counterterrorist operations are significantly different from those required in predominantly rural settings and also significantly different from those of ordinary police work. For example, effective urban counterterrorism operations rely on strong intelligence-gathering and tactical control of neighborhoods in which municipal authorities have little real presence. In a Pashtun *kachi abadi* of Karachi, for example, local police would be unable to speak the inhabitants' language, immediately identifiable as outsiders, and potentially outgunned by the Taliban-affiliated power brokers who maintain effective control of the shantytown. For the past decade, the central government's counterterrorist units have largely focused on operations in sparsely populated parts of FATA: The resources and training needed to assault an isolated rural compound differ markedly from those needed to capture a suspect in a teeming city bazaar.

Demographic Shifts Are Likely to Make Karachi a Potential Site for Increased Terrorism and Anti-American Extremist Operations

The prevalence of terrorism and violent militancy in Karachi is hardly a new phenomenon. Any city this large, diverse, and unruly will attract its share of criminals, radicals, and underworld facilitators. Al Qaeda leaders Khalid Sheikh Muhammad and Ramzi bin al-Shibh both operated out of Karachi for long periods, and American journalist Daniel Pearl was kidnapped and beheaded there. Underworld king-pin Dawood Ibrahim, believed to have operational ties to Lashkar-e-Taiba, is reported to divide his time between Dubai and Karachi. In the future, demographic shifts in Karachi may further encourage terrorists to take up residence in Pakistan's largest city.

For the past three decades, political violence and organized crime in Karachi operated under the aegis of MQM. That is not to say that MQM was itself responsible for most violence (although it was, and is, responsible for a considerable amount of it) but that, as the wielder of political power and law enforcement, MQM set the parameters for what types of criminal activity might or might not provoke a sustained police response. MQM—secular and oriented toward Urdu-speaking Mohajirs rather than Pashtuns or Punjabis—is not a natural ally of terrorist or militant groups, such as Al Qaeda, Lashkar-e-Taiba, or the Haqqani Network. Indeed, it has a strong interest in preventing such groups from operating freely in Karachi. Demographic trends suggest that MQM's hold on Karachi will slip over time: The number of Mohajirs is essentially static or declining, while the number of Pashtuns and other communities entering Karachi is growing. As Karachi gets more demographically diverse and politically chaotic, more space may open for a wide variety of terrorist groups.

In the years preceding the most recent elections, Pashtun migrants to Karachi tended to find their political voice through the secular ANP. This trend, however, did not hold true for the 2013 polls and may weaken further in the future. In 2013, ANP demonstrated remarkable weakness even in its KPK power base. In Karachi, as elsewhere, ANP lost ground to Pashtun-oriented groups linked to the Tehrik-e Taliban Pakistan, the Quetta Shura Taliban, or parties with multiethnic appeal, such as PTI. In urban settings, the advantages that political parties hold in being able to distribute patronage help provide a strong rational incentive for voters to align with a party contesting for national, provincial, or local rule. ANP may not yet be out of the game: A failure to improve quality of life could cause PTI, TTP, and other groups to lose the Pashtun support they garnered in 2013. But unless

ANP gets better at delivering concrete benefits to its Pashtun constituents and operating under the threat of TTP violence, some Taliban groups' centers of gravity may shift from the border areas into parts of Pakistan's largest city in the near future.

Demographic Shifts Are Less Likely to Produce Such Outcomes in Lahore or Quetta

The demography of Lahore and Quetta, for different reasons, is unlikely to reproduce the dynamic of Karachi in either city. Lahore is now, and is likely to remain in the future, an overwhelmingly Punjabi city—internal migrants have tended to head for Karachi rather than Lahore. Quetta, on the other hand, has already shifted from a majority-Baloch to a plurality Pashtun city, with a sizable Hazara minority; both the Pashtun and Hazara immigrations were fueled by war in Afghanistan, with large waves coming in 1996, 2001, and at other moments of heightened conflict across the Durand Line. Additional shifts of population balance may well lie in the future, but the key demographic shift in Quetta (Baloch to Pashtun plurality) has already occurred.

Violent actors are not absent from either city: Lahore remains the de facto headquarters for Lashkar-e-Taiba, and Quetta remains the home of the Quetta Shura Taliban. Other terrorist and militant groups operate in both cities. But the drivers for increased (or decreased) terrorist activity in both cities will likely be factors other than demographics: In both cities, the attitude of civilian and military authorities is likely to be more determinative than the social makeup of the cities.

Demography and Urbanization Are Unlikely to Dislodge the PML-N/PPP Duopoly from Control of Pakistan's Central Government and Most Provincial Governments

As discussed above, Pakistan's civilian government will likely remain in the hands of the two major parties for the foreseeable future. In security terms, this means that the future is likely to show greater continuity than discontinuity with the past. When in office, both PML-N and the PPP can be expected to be problematic friends—but ultimately to strive to avoid a rupture in relations with the United States and to take U.S. security concerns into serious consideration. When in opposition, both parties can be expected to trumpet anti-U.S. rhetoric, along with every other political party. Neither PML-N nor PPP can be considered a close "friend" of the United States, and neither can be considered an enemy. And regardless of which party is in power at a given time, the locus of key security decisions will remain the Pakistani military establishment.

Demography and Urbanization Are Unlikely to Bring Islamist Parties to Power at the Center or in Punjab and Sindh

Such demographic trends as rural-urban migration (especially from Pashtun areas), increased flow of war and postconflict refugees (from Afghanistan and from FATA/KPK), and return of Pakistanis working in the Gulf all *potentially* serve to bolster the political power of Islamist parties; this is true in the border regions and, to a lesser extent, in the major Sindhi and Punjabi cities. So far, however, this has been more of a *potential* development than an *actual* one. Despite many years of predictions to the contrary, Islamist parties remain far removed from gaining lasting power at the national level; even at the provincial or municipal level, they have yet to make real inroads in major population centers (that is, at the provincial level in Punjab and Sindh, at the municipal level in any of the eight most populous cities).

There are signs of increased success by the Islamist parties in the border areas. In the 2013 elections, for example, the secular Pashtun-based party ANP lost ground to the Islamist Pashtun-based party JUI-F: In KPK (its power base), ANP won fewer than one-third as many provincial assembly seats (four seats for ANP, 13 for JUI-F); it lost out even to the Punjab-based Islamist party JI (which won seven seats). But that is not the entire picture. The biggest winner in KPK was not an Islamist party but another secular party—the reformist (and

Punjab-based) PTI, which won 35 seats; even the secular Punjab-based PML-N, which had previously been a nonfactor there, won nearly as many seats (12) as JUI-F. Another secular party (the Qoumi Watan Party, an offshoot of the PPP) won the same number of seats as JI, and yet another secular party (Awami Jamhuri Ittehad Pakistan) won three. In the Balochistan provincial assembly, JUI-F won six seats—but secular parties won almost all of the rest: National parties PML-N and PML-Q won nine and five seats; the Pashtun-based Pakistan PMAP won ten, the ANP won one; and the Baloch-based National Party and Baloch National Party won seven and two, respectively.[5]

In terms of U.S. security interests, an electoral victory by Pakistan's Islamist parties would not necessarily translate into radical shifts in policy. JUI-F, the most successful of the Islamist parties (and often the most fiery in its denunciation of American policies) has been a frequent coalition ally of the secular, center-left PPP at the center (including in the previous National Assembly). Hard-line ideology does not necessarily result in hard-line policy—and is frequently outweighed by political expedience.

Demography and Urbanization Are Likely to Increase Popular Demand for Political Reform—With Both Positive and Potentially Adverse Impacts on U.S. Security Interests

One trend that can be confidently predicted is the continued popular demand for better governance. Nearly all sections of Pakistani society feel this hunger, but the march of urbanization and the associated demographic trends have given it fresh political power. While prior generations of disenfranchised rural citizens might have suffered in silence, their children are less and less likely to do so.

In the 2013 election, PTI served as an effective vehicle for widespread frustration felt by tens of millions of Pakistani voters, but the

---

[5] HamariWeb.com, 2013.

party is a beneficiary of the reform movement rather than its driver.[6] Unless it is able to establish a track record of successful governance on which to base its future campaigns, PTI may falter. The party lacks a demographic base, an active group of party workers, and a coherent ideology: A successful party can be built on one of the three of these foundations (ideally, all three), but it will have a difficult time establishing itself without at least one. The rhetoric Imran Khan expresses is in tune with the sentiments of many voters—probably a solid majority of voters in most constituencies. He rails against the corruption of the political establishment (both PPP and PML-N), excesses of the military (although he is careful not to push the point too far), and—most strenuously—against U.S. actions, from drone strikes in FATA to foreign troops in Afghanistan to CIA and Special Operations Forces action throughout Pakistan. But such rhetoric is little different from that of Pakistani politicians of all parties: The main distinctions are Khan's personal charisma and the fact that he (unlike PML-N or PPP politicians) is untainted by ever having held a ministerial office. As of this writing, Khan has not brought significant reform to the government of KPK and has not translated his fiery anti-U.S. rhetoric into concrete action.[7] Despite repeated promises to shut down the ground lines of communication for NATO supplies to Afghanistan in protest of drone attacks, Khan has yet to prevent a single vehicle from crossing Torkham Gate.[8] In short, the PTI may or may not pose a long-term threat to the two major parties—but the widespread desire for reform is unlikely to go away.

From a U.S. security perspective, this has both positive and negative aspects. The negative aspects are most visible in the near and medium terms: It may well become more difficult for Pakistani lead-

---

[6]   For discussion of Pakistan's prior movements for governmental reform and accountability, along with the impact of these movements on development, see Jonah Blank, "Democratization and Development," in Devin T. Haggerty, ed., *South Asia in World Politics*, Lanham, Md.: Rowman and Littlefield, 2005, pp. 231–256.

[7]   As this report goes to press, the outcome of late-summer 2014 PTI-led protests against the government of Nawaz Sharif remains undetermined.

[8]   Salman Masood and Ihsanullah Tipu Mehsud, "Thousands in Pakistan Protest American Drone Strikes," *New York Times*, November 23, 2013.

ers to pursue policies (such as tacit support for U.S. drone strikes) that are highly unpopular. In past decades, Pakistani leaders (military and civilian alike) were able to ignore public opinion on national security issues as long as they could maintain the support of the corps commanders. Such a luxury may soon be a thing of the past.

For the long term, however, the positive aspects of this trend may outweigh the negative aspects, even from the perspective of U.S. security interests alone. Much of the anti-American sentiment in Pakistan can be seen as a redirection of popular anger flowing from political disenfranchisement and poor governance. If this analysis is correct, the reform movement is a Pakistani solution to a Pakistani problem—but one from which the United States will eventually be a collateral beneficiary.

One of the key questions about Pakistani politics that policymakers often ask is what effect demographic shifts are likely to have on the impact of Islamist parties. Our analysis suggests that Islamist parties (whether Salafist or Deobandi) are unlikely to become the dominant force in Pakistani politics in the foreseeable future and are unlikely even to provide the framework within which other parties will operate. Islamist ideology is not an overwhelming impediment to political success but is insufficient to overcome a lack of perceived governing competence. This could change if Islamist parties start developing governing ability, either in national ministries, as members of broader coalitions, or through experience administering municipal or provincial governments. Constituent service—in other words, good governance—may be the most effective electoral strategy for whichever Pakistani party might choose to adopt it. While individual voters are likely to prefer good governance, powerful elites continue to benefit from the old system, and it is these elites that will resist change using violence, money, and other resource advantages they garner from the current governing arrangement. Good governance does not fail at the ballot box; good governance fails because the ballot box is only one among many means of apportioning power in Pakistani society.

CHAPTER SIX

Lessons for the Future

Conclusions

To summarize the above analysis, how will urbanization affect politics and political stability in Pakistan? The following points ought to be stressed:

Urbanization in general, and its specific demographic patterns in Pakistan, may serve to fuel anti-American sentiment and complicate U.S. counterterrorism operations in the near and medium terms.

Ethnic-based non-Islamist parties (of most direct note, MQM and ANP) do not appear to be benefiting significantly from demographic shifts. In the case of MQM, the demographic shifts work decidedly against their core base of support: Few Mohajirs will migrate into Karachi (or, for that matter, other Pakistani cities) in the future, whether from villages or from smaller urban centers, while there will be a steady outflow of Mohajirs to the UK, the United States, and other international destinations. For ANP, the limiting factor is not demography but ideology: While ANP has historically dominated the political pool of Pashtuns from KPK, it is in increasingly tough competition with JUI-F and other Pashtun-oriented parties with more-powerful ideological platforms (and, in the 2013 election, even with the non-Pashtun-based PTI and PML-N). In an era when all parties have adopted rhetoric opposing U.S. involvement in Pakistan, supporting Islamic identity at home, and championing Muslim causes abroad, ANP's more-secular approach might appear out of step with the electorate. As increasing numbers of Pashtuns migrate to large cities and work overseas (especially in the Gulf) for extended periods, their party loyalties will be determined less by family tradition and more by their current concerns.

Urbanization weakens both of the two mainstream parties to a degree. Both PML-N and PPP have traditionally relied on feudal vote-banks for a significant number of their parliamentary seats. To the extent that urbanization increases the number of voters who might actually show up at the polls, the trend decreases the ability of the two largest parties simply to pile up seats by tending to the interests of rural power brokers. The stranglehold of these two main parties over Pakistani politics, which reached its height in the 1990s, may not be the pattern of the future.

It bears remembering, however, that this paradigm of a secularist two-party system in Pakistan is *not* the historical norm. Before the 2008 election, the structure under which the PPP and PML traded turns in office had lasted only a decade (1989–1999). Most of Pakistan's history has been that of one-party (i.e., PML) dominance during periods of de facto or de jure military rule, punctuated by an uncharacteristic period (1971–1977) of one-party (i.e., PPP) dominance in a brief era of meaningful civilian leadership. The duopoly is likely to last for the immediate future but is by no means predestined to last forever. With that said, there is a strong empirical finding in comparative politics that first-past-the-post systems are associated with a reduction in the number of viable parties (so-called Duverger's Law), though this tendency can be overwhelmed by geographic concentration of ethnic or other identity groups.

One vital element undergirds all calculations about Pakistani politics: the military's role. The PPP government elected in 2008 ended its term of office with very low public approval ratings—but it was also the only civilian government in Pakistani history to serve out its full term. Had other civilian regimes been permitted a full term of office, they too might have thoroughly disenchanted even their core supporters. A large part of the reason that no political party has been able to make good on its promises is that the Pakistani military has not permitted any party to do so: The implicit threat of a coup has hung over every government, and the army has put its thumb on the scale of elections repeatedly in Pakistani history. The military has occasionally permitted outcomes it has not seen as ideal but has seldom permitted, and in the foreseeable future remains unlikely to permit, any outcome it considers to be counter to its core institutional interests.

Projections on the Course of Pakistani Politics

Demography Is Not Destiny
None of the potential claimants currently on the scene—PTI, PML-Q, JUI-F, ANP, MQM, JI, or any possible combination of these elements and their core constituencies—seems likely to overturn the PPP/PML-N duopoly in the near future. Both PPP and PML-N will have to rule as part of broader coalitions. These coalitions will shape Pakistani politics, but it is likely that these coalitions will form and reshuffle on the basis of political expediency rather than bedrock ideological differences. Most of the parties will be affected positively or adversely by demographic shifts in Pakistan's major cities, but these shifts will not transform the political map in the near or medium term. It is not difficult to envision virtually any of the smaller political parties allying with either of the two largest ones in a marriage of electoral convenience—and equally easy to imagine any of these unions leading to an electoral divorce.

There Are No Game-Changers on the Horizon
PML-N and PPP remain basically the same parties they have been for decades, and neither shows any sign of making significant ideological changes. Whether one of them emerges as a truly dominant, enduring force (rather than merely the lesser of two evils in the eyes of Pakistani voters) will depend not on ideology but on whether it is consistently able to deliver concrete results (electricity, education, jobs, physical security) to a critical mass of the electorate.

The X-Factor in the Equation Is Popular Demand for Governance
There is a deep hunger throughout the Pakistani electorate for something more than the current choices. The two most recent attempts to fill this vacuum have been the PTI and the "Long March" by the

cleric Muhammad Tahir-ul Qadri. The first is a party led by a long-time London sybarite and, in the nearly two decades prior to 2013, managed to elect exactly one member of parliament. The second was a short-lived protest movement, led by a cleric of dual Canadian-Pakistani citizenship, that has never elected even a single member.[1] The fact that Pakistani citizens have been drawn to such improbable figures—and the fact that Imran Khan's party garnered 16.7 percent of the vote in the May 2013 elections—demonstrates the depth of popular alienation from the two established parties.

This hunger for good governance is an issue for rural and urban voters alike. From the smallest hamlet in Baltistan right up to the teeming streets of Karachi, most Pakistani citizens have little faith in their political leaders. The percentage of Pakistanis who ascribe "somewhat good" or "very good" influence for Pakistan to the national government has declined dramatically since Pew began asking the question in 2002 (see Figure 6.1).[2] Additionally, the percentage of Pakistanis who perceive corruption of political leaders as a major problem has increased from a vast majority in 2002 to near universal consensus in more recent years (see Figure 6.2).

Few Pakistanis would argue with the proposition that politicians of all stripes have failed to address the basic issues of governance (see Figures 6.1 and 6.2), but patterns of urbanization give this near-universal sentiment an added saliency. As Pakistan's voters increasingly congregate in densely packed and information-saturated urban environments, they will become increasingly unwilling to accept unsatisfactory performance from their leaders.

---

[1] In January 2013, Tahir-ul Qadri initiated what he termed a "Million Man March" from Lahore to Islamabad. Participation was estimated to have been far short of the projected number, and the movement soon faded. In August 2014, both Imran Khan and Tahir-ul Qadri launched a series of anticorruption rallies, with an impact that (as of the date of publication of this report) remains uncertain.

[2] Pew Research Center, Global Attitudes Project, 2012.

Figure 6.1
Perceived Impact of National Government on Own Lives

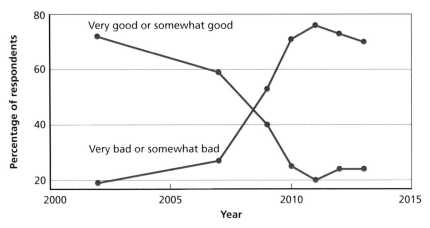

SOURCE: Pew Research Center, Global Attitudes Project, 2013.
NOTE: Question was phrased: "As I read a list of groups and organizations, for each, please tell me what kind of influence the group is having on the way things are going in Pakistan: a. our national government."
RAND RR644-6.1

Figure 6.2
Pakistani Views of Corruption

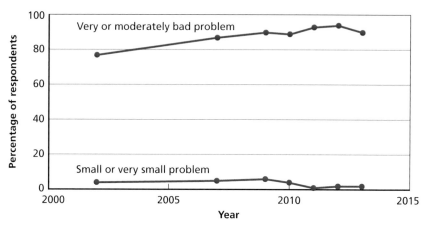

SOURCE: Pew Research Center, Global Attitudes Project, 2013.
NOTE: Question was phrased: "Now I am going to read you a list of things that may
be problems in our country. Tell me if you think it is a very big problem, a moderately
big problem, a small problem or not a problem at all: b. corrupt political leaders."
RAND *RR644-6.2*

APPENDIX

Most Populous Cities

Table A.1
Top 50 Most Populous Cities in Pakistan

Rank	City	Population (2015 UN est.)	Population (1998 census)	Province
1	Karachi	15,500,000	9,339,023	Sindh
2	Lahore	8,491,000	5,143,495	Punjab
3	Faisalabad	3,434,000	2,008,861	Punjab
4	Rawalpindi	2,453,000	1,409,768	Punjab
5	Multan	2,014,000	1,197,384	Punjab
6	Gujranwala	2,006,000	1,132,509	Punjab
7	Hyderabad	1,931,000	1,166,894	Sindh
8	Peshawar	1,730,000	982,816	KPK
9	Islamabad	1,049,000	529,180	Islamabad Capital Territory
10	Quetta	1,030,000	565,137	Balochistan
11	Sargodha	—	458,440	Punjab
12	Sialkot	—	421,502	Punjab
13	Bahawalpur	—	408,395	Punjab
14	Sukkur	—	335,551	Sindh
15	Jhang	—	293,366	Punjab
16	Shekhupura	—	280,263	Punjab
17	Larkana	—	270,283	Sindh
18	Gujrat	—	251,792	Punjab

Table A.1—Continued

Rank	City	Population (2015 UN est.)	Population (1998 census)	Province
19	Mardan	—	245,926	KPK
20	Kasur	—	245,321	Punjab
21	Rahim Yar Khan	—	233,537	Punjab
22	Sahiwal	—	208,778	Punjab
23	Okara	—	201,815	Punjab
24	Wah Cantonment	—	198,431	Punjab
25	Dera Ghazi Khan	—	188,149	Punjab
26	Mirpur Khas	—	184,465	Sindh
27	Nawabshah	—	183,110	Sindh
28	Mingora	—	174,469	KPK
29	Chiniot	—	169,282	Punjab
30	Kamoke	—	150,984	Punjab
31	Burewala	—	149,857	Punjab
32	Jhelum	—	145,847	Punjab
33	Sadiqabad	—	141,509	Punjab
34	Jacobabad	—	137,733	Sindh
35	Shikarpur	—	133,259	Sindh
36	Khanewal	—	132,962	Punjab
37	Hafizabad	—	130,216	Punjab
38	Kohat	—	125,271	KPK
39	Muzaffargarh	—	121,641	Punjab
40	Khanpur	—	117,764	Punjab
41	Gojra	—	114,967	Punjab
42	Bahawalnagar	—	109,642	Punjab
43	Muridke	—	108,578	Punjab
44	Pakpattan	—	107,791	Punjab
45	Abbottabad	—	105,999	KPK
46	Tando Adam	—	103,363	Sindh

Table A.1—Continued

Rank	City	Population (2015 UN est.)	Population (1998 census)	Province
47	Jaranwala	—	103,308	Punjab
48	Khairpur	—	102,188	Sindh
49	Chishtian	—	101,659	Punjab
50	Daska	—	101,500	Punjab

SOURCES: UN Population Division data as of April 29, 2014; Population Census Organization, 1998; Brinkhoff, undated.

References

Andrés, Luis, Dan Biller, and Matías Herrera Dappe, *Reducing Poverty by Closing South Asia's Infrastructure Gap,* Washington, D.C.: The World Bank, December 2013.

Ashfaque, Azfar-ul, "Impact on Karachi Politics," *Dawn* (Pakistan), December 26, 2011.

Asian Development Bank, *Karachi Mega Cities Preparation Project: Final Report*, Vol. 1, August 2005. As of August 27, 2014:
http://www2.adb.org/Documents/Produced-Under-TA/38405/38405-PAK-DPTA.pdf

Blank, Jonah, "Democratization and Development," in Devin T. Haggerty, ed., *South Asia in World Politics*, Lanham, Md.: Rowman and Littlefield, 2005, pp. 231–256.

———, "Kashmir: All Tactics, No Strategy," in Sumit Ganguly, ed., *The Kashmir Question: Retrospect and Prospect*, London: Frank Cass, 2003, pp. 181–202.

———, "Kashmir: Fundamentalism Takes Root." *Foreign Affairs*, Vol. 78, No. 6 November/December 1999, pp. 36–53. As of June 26, 2014:
http://www.foreignaffairs.com/articles/55602/jonah-blank/kashmir-fundamentalism-takes-root

———, "Lashkar-e-Taiba and the Threat to the United States of a Mumbai-Style Attack," testimony delivered to the House of Representatives Committee on Homeland Security, Subcommittee on Counterterrorism and Intelligence, Santa Monica, Calif.: RAND Corporation, CT-390, June 12, 2013. As of July 31, 2014:
http://www.rand.org/pubs/testimonies/CT390.html

———, *Mullahs on the Mainframe: Islam and Modernity Among the Daudi Bohras*, Chicago: University of Chicago Press, 2001.

Brinkhoff, Thomas, "Pakistan," City Population website, undated. As of April 29, 2014:
http://www.citypopulation.de/Pakistan-20T.html

Electoral Commission of Pakistan, "Detailed Position of Political Parties/Alliances in National Assembly General Elections," 2002. As of January 22, 2010: http://www.ecp.gov.pk/content/GE-2002.htm

———, "Party Wise Vote Bank," May 27, 2013. As of April 3, 2014: http://ecp.gov.pk/Misc2013/voteBank.pdf

Fair, C. Christine, testimony before the U.S. House of Representatives Committee on Foreign Affairs, Subcommittee on Oversight and Investigations, February 8, 2012. As of August 27, 2014: http://home.comcast.net/~christine_fair/pubs/20120208_Testimony_Fair_Balochistan.pdf

Ganguly, Sumit, ed., *The Kashmir Question: Retrospect and Prospect*. London: Frank Cass, 2003.

Gazdar, Haris, "Karachi Demographic and Politics," presentation of the Urban Resource Center, Karachi, November 6, 2013. As of April 30, 2014: http://www.urckarachi.org/Karachi%20Demographic%20and%20politics%20Presentation%20by%20Haris%20Gazdar.pptx

Gazdar, Haris, Sobia Ahmad Kaker, and Irfan Khan, *Buffer Zone or Urban Hub? Quetta: Between Four Regions and Two Wars,* working paper, London: Crisis States Research Centre, London School of Economics, 2010.

Ghumman, Khawar, "Aliens in Karachi: No Significant Change in Statistics," *Dawn* (Pakistan), February 23, 2014.

Haggerty, Devin T., ed., *South Asia in World Politics*, Lanham, Md.: Rowman and Littlefield, 2005.

HamariWeb.com (Pakistani election news website), 2013. As of July 31, 2014: http://hamariweb.com/pakistan-election-2013/

Hasan, Arif, "The Impending Migration," *Dawn* (Pakistan), December 4, 2012.

International Republican Institute, "IRI Index: Pakistan Public Opinion Survey, November 19–28, 2007. As of July 31, 2014: http://www.iri.org/sites/default/files/2007-12-12-pakistan-poll.pdf

———, "Detailed Methodology: Survey of Pakistan Public Opinion, February 9–March 3, 2012," April 23, 2012. As of August 27, 2014: http://www.iri.org/news-events-press-center/news/detailed-methodology-survey-pakistan-pulic-opinion-february-9-march-3-

Iqbal, Anwar, "PTI Losing Ground Amid PML-N Surge: IRI survey," *Dawn* (Pakistan), September 30, 2012. As of August 27, 2014: http://www.dawn.com/news/753057/pti-losing-ground-amid-pml-n-surge-iri-survey

IRI—*See* International Republican Institute.

Jan, Bahrawar, Mohammad Iqbal, and Iftikharuddin, "Urbanization Trends and Urban Population Projection of Pakistan Using Weighted Approach," *Sarhad Journal of Agriculture*, Vol. 24, No. 1, 2008, pp. 173–180.

Lieven, Anatol, *Pakistan: A Hard Country*, New York: Public Affairs, 2011.

Maher, Mahim, "Demography and Migrations: The Curious Case of Karachi's Ghost Population," *The Express Tribune* (Pakistan), March 29, 2014.

Masood, Salman, and Ihsanullah Tipu Mehsud, "Thousands in Pakistan Protest American Drone Strikes," *New York Times*, November 23, 2013. As of November 27, 2013:
http://www.nytimes.com/2013/11/24/world/asia/in-pakistan-rally-protests-drone-strikes.html

Mustafa, Daanish, and Amiera Sawas, "Urbanization and Political Change in Pakistan: Exploring the Known Unknowns," draft, London: King's College, 2012.

National Assembly of Pakistan, "Pakistan Tehreek-e-Insaf (PTI) Seats Distribution," 2014a. As of April 30, 2014:
http://www.na.gov.pk/en/members_listing.php?party=103

———, "Pukhtoonkhwa Milli Awami Party (PMAP) Seats Distribution," 2014b. As of May 3, 2014:
http://www.na.gov.pk/en/members_listing.php?party=108

Pakistan Bureau of Statistics, Government of Pakistan, "Pakistan Social and Living Standards Measurement: Brief on Pakistan Social & Living Standard Measurement (PSLM) Survey 2004–15," website, undated. As of December 2, 2013:
http://www.pbs.gov.pk/content/pakistan-social-and-living-standards-measurement

Pew Research Center, Global Attitudes Project. "Pakistani Public Opinion Ever More Critical of U.S.; 74% Call America an Enemy," Washington, D.C., June 27, 2012.

———, "2013 Spring Survey Topline Results," May 7, 2013. As of July 31, 2014:
http://www.pewglobal.org/files/2013/05/Pew-Global-Attitudes-Pakistan-Topline-FINAL-May-7-2013.pdf

"Pindi Police Nab 16 Afghan Nationals Under Foreign Act," *Daily Times* (Pakistan), February 24, 2014.

Population Census Organization, Government of Pakistan, "Population Size and Growth of Major Cities," 1998. As of April 29, 2014:
http://www.census.gov.pk/MajorCities.htm

Population Census Organization, Statistics Division, Government of Pakistan, *Quetta: Population and Housing Census, 1998*, Islamabad: Government of Pakistan, 2003.

Population Census Organization, Statistics Division, Government of Pakistan, *Lahore: Population and Housing Census, 1998*, Islamabad: Government of Pakistan, 2004a.

Population Census Organization, *Karachi City: Population and Housing Census, 1998*, Islamabad: Government of Pakistan, 2004b.

Population Census Organization, "Everyone Counts: Census 2011," Islamabad: Government of Pakistan, 2011. As of September 9, 2014:
http://census.gov.pk/census2011.php

Provincial Assembly of Punjab, "Member's Directory: By Party Affiliation," 2014. As of April 30, 2014:
http://www.pap.gov.pk/index.php/members/party_pos/en/20

Provincial Assembly of Sindh, "Members' List for: Pakistan Tehreek-e-Insaf," 2014. As of April 30, 2014:
http://www.pas.gov.pk/index.php/members/byparty/en/31/32

Provincial Assembly of Balochistan, "By District: Quetta," 2014. As of May 3, 2014:
http://www.pabalochistan.gov.pk/index.php/members/bydistrict/en/27/248

"PTI Senior Leader Killed on Eve of Karachi Polls," *Dawn* (Pakistan), May 19, 2013.

Rehman, Zia-ur, "Swing Seats," *The Friday Times* (Pakistan), April 26, 2013.

Shahid, Saleem, "Cracks but No Sign of Break-Up," *Dawn* (Pakistan), February 15, 2014.

———, "PkMAP, PML-N Eye Quetta Mayor's Post," *Dawn* (Pakistan), December 18, 2013.

UN—*See* United Nations.

UNHCR—*See* United Nations High Commissioner for Refugees.

United Nations, Department of Economic and Social Affairs, Population Division, *World Urbanization Prospects: The 2011 Revision*, 2012. As of November 29, 2013:
http://esa.un.org/unup/pdf/WUP2011_Highlights.pdf

United Nations, Department of Economic and Social Affairs, Population Division, Population Estimates and Projects Section, "On-Line Data: Urban and Rural Population," database, 2014. As of February 21, 2014:
http://esa.un.org/unpd/wup/unup/index_panel1.html

———, "On-Line Data: Urban Agglomerations," database, 2014. As of February 21, 2014:
http://esa.un.org/unpd/wup/unup/index_panel2.html

————, "On-Line Data: Country Profiles," database, 2014. As of February 21, 2014:
http://esa.un.org/unpd/wup/unup/index_panel3.html

United Nations High Commissioner for Refugees, "2014 UNHCR Country Operations Profile—Pakistan," 2014. As of May 2, 2014:
http://www.unhcr.org/pages/49e487016.html

Varshney, Ashutosh, *Ethnic Conflict and Civic Life*, New Haven: Yale University Press, 2002.

White, Joshua T., "Conflicted Islamisms: Shariah, Decision-Making, and Anti-State Agitation Among Pakistani Islamist Parties," PhD thesis, Washington, D.C.: Johns Hopkins School of Advanced International Studies, July 2013.

World Bank, *Migration and Remittances Factbook, 2011*. As of November 29, 2013:
http://data.worldbank.org/data-catalog/migration-and-remittances

————, "Bilateral Migration and Remittances," *Prospects*, undated. As of May 1, 2014:
http://go.worldbank.org/JITC7NYTT0

Yusuf, Farhat, "Size and Sociodemographic Characteristics of the Afghan Refugee Population in Pakistan," *Journal of Biosocial Science*, Vol. 22, No. 3, July 1990, pp. 269–279.